Searching for the

Indigenous Church

A Missionary Pilgrimage

Searching for the

Indigenous Church

A Missionary Pilgrimage

Gene Daniels

William Carey Library
Pasadena, California
www.WCLBooks.com

Cover design: Joseph Gil

Editing and book design: Sharon Edwards

Published by William Carey Library
1605 E. Elizabeth Street
Pasadena, California 91104
www.WCLBooks.com

William Carey Library is a Ministry of the
U.S. Center for World Mission, Pasadena, California.

ISBN 0-87808-343-X

Second printing – February 2006

Printed in the United States of America

Dedicated to...

My dear wife Linda
and our four wonderful children,
who suffered to live with me through countless rewrites.

My fellow pilgrim,
"Uncle Lenin" (you know who you are),
who encouraged me to never give up this magnificent search.

The many brothers and sisters in Central Asia,
whose love and friendship
have blessed my family beyond measure.
Without these servants of Christ
this book would never have been written.
Therefore, it is especially to them
that I would like to dedicate the following pages.

CONTENTS

Foreword   *ix*

Preface   *xiii*

Prologue: *A Heart Set on Pilgrimage*   1

Chapter 1:   *Land of the Steppe*   11

Chapter 2:   *Point of Entry*   19

Chapter 3:   *Shrines*   33

Chapter 4:   *Caravansary*   43

Chapter 5:   *On Being Lost*   51

Chapter 6:   *Signs in the Sky*   75

Chapter 7:   *A Late Night Challenge*   81

Chapter 8:   *Labin's Long Shadow*   93

Chapter 9:   *Funerals*   101

Chapter 10:   *Hassan's Advice*   113

Chapter 11:   *Tea Party Terrorists*   127

Chapter 12:   *Wind, Sand, and Time*   135

Chapter 13:   *Poplar Trees*   145

Chapter 14:   *A Time for Everything*   155

Epilogue: *The Treasures in My Bag*   169

Scripture Cited   177

FOREWORD

The central goal in missions is the establishment of strong, growing indigenous churches. Gene Daniels addresses that crucial subject in the pages of this remarkable book.

This book is remarkable because of the way in which the author communicates his experiences as a church planter. He takes the reader along with him on a journey—a pilgrimage—to Central Asia, vividly describing the challenges and pitfalls encountered by cross-cultural workers en route. We, the readers, take a "virtual" trip to plant an indigenous church in a foreign land with him and learn from his frustrations and difficulties.

Many books have been written about the problems associated with crossing into another culture. Most of them are helpful, indeed valuable, but they do not quite prepare the reader for his or her actual arrival in a cross-cultural setting. No matter how much we have read about the need to remove our culturally tinted glasses and see things from the perspective of another culture, most of us have great difficulty doing so. The main reason for this is that we don't even recognize we are wearing such glasses.

Gene Daniels makes us aware of our cultural glasses more effectively than any author I know. For this reason alone I believe his book is *must* reading for anyone contemplating missionary service—in Central Asia or elsewhere.

I have another reason for recommending this book: it is a pleasure to read. Gene Daniels is a talented writer and *Searching for the Indigenous Church* is one of the best-written missionary books I have read. The reader feels that he or she is experiencing the author's pilgrimage firsthand. Daniels' insights are sharp; his observations, telling. I have felt both challenged and edified by reading this book.

The author rightly focuses on the "planting" aspects of establishing an indigenous church, but he acknowledges that there is more to establishing an indigenous church than just planting it. The seed needs to be watered. The discipling of new believers is essential if a new church is to grow and become strong; missionaries have an important role here also.

Shortly before I began my own missionary pilgrimage in 1970, I was given a list of eight essential books to read on the subject of missions. Perhaps the best way I can endorse Gene Daniels' book is to say that I deeply wish it had been included in my reading list back in 1970. It would have helped me be a more effective missionary.

Thomas Hale

Author, *On Being a Missionary*

and *A Light Shines in Central Asia*

*N*o book has ever been the exclusive product of one person's genius. Rather, the author, via interaction with countless others, develops a unique perspective on the world which they later attempt to bring to the printed page. And so it is in this case; this book is unquestionably the echo of many other voices who have contributed without knowing it.

As if that did not make the matter of giving credit hard enough, there is an additional concern in this case— security. My pilgrimage has been through an active and ongoing missionary work in Muslim lands where those who profess Christ are watched suspiciously by neighbor and government alike. So for the sake of all concerned, I have carefully guarded locations and names.

However, I can promise the reader that everything I describe really did happen. And if at times you are tempted to doubt this, remember, Jesus blessed those who had eyes that see, ears that hear, and hearts willing to comprehend.

PROLOGUE

A Heart Set on Pilgrimage

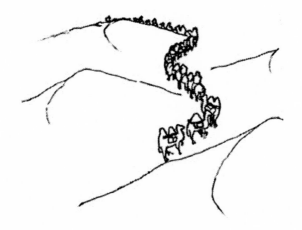

$\mathcal{F}$rom the beginning of the practice of religions, people have from time to time left the comfort of home and traveled to remote places for spiritual reasons. While it is true that all of us have mixed motivations, most of those who have made these difficult journeys have done so as an expression of a deep and sacred devotion.

From the Genesis account of Abraham's three-day journey to Mt. Moriah, to the medieval pilgrims depicted in *The Canterbury Tales*, to the modern-day Islamic pilgrims who flow into Mecca by the millions each year, devout people the world over express their piety through a pilgrimage.

This longing was immortalized in the words of the sons of Korah:

How lovely is your dwelling place, O LORD Almighty!
My soul yearns, even faints for the courts of the LORD…

Blessed are those whose strength is in you,
who have set their hearts on pilgrimage…
Better is one day in your courts,
than a thousand elsewhere.

According to the Vatican's definition, the word *pilgrimage* carries the idea of "wandering over a distance." Pilgrimages therefore may be defined as "journeys made to some place with the purpose of venerating it, or to discharge some religious obligation."

I don't quite have the weight of the Pope backing me, but I have spent a great deal of time meditating on this subject while on a journey of my own. For you see, I too have been on a pilgrimage of sorts—a missionary pilgrimage in Central Asia.

When I started this journey, I thought that world mission was about stuff like gospel radio, printing presses, and progress. And for many it is, for missions is surely a vast arena. But we will not concern ourselves with the scores of noble and progressive things that missionaries often do; nor will we address the complexities they face in the process. Rather, we are on a search for only one thing—a simple little miracle we call the *indigenous church.*

To some it may sound strange to begin a book about the indigenous church, a major tenet of the modern missions movement, in the medieval language of pilgrimage. And indeed, it is strange.

But then again, anything that *really* has to do with the indigenous church will be strange to us as foreign missionaries. Its fabric, if truly indigenous, is cut from a cloth of a different color. It is woven to patterns we often do not like or understand. In fact, these are usually the very things that make it indigenous.

The drama of seeing God weave His story in the hearts of a new people and culture often has very little to do with the things we Westerners value so highly. Maybe that is why many missionaries prefer things such as gospel radio and printing presses? Things we can control. Things we can understand.

The modern evangelical missions movement was birthed in a time of intellect and education—an age of reason, if you will. We have come to believe that with enough study, we can understand, define, and therefore control anything, even those things that are intrinsically incomprehensible to us.

So, in the prevailing attitude of our culture, the indigenous church has been studied and analyzed in literally hundreds of articles and books during the past few decades. Great churchmen, missions scholars, and even simple field practitioners like myself have written about this elusive goal.

Acronyms have been formulated so we will remember its main features. Multiplied numbers of methodologies have been taught that seem to almost guarantee an indigenous church as their result—if we follow them exactly.

You might say that the indigenous church has become a sort of Holy Grail for many of us. Like the pious adventurers of old, we launch out from our homelands, bravely going forth to difficult, even dangerous places, to seek this grand treasure.

To be able to report back home that we have planted one indigenous church, however we might define it, would be phenomenal. Such a tale would inspire awe, and it would bring renewed financial support from our home churches. It would stir the heart, as did the stories told by those weary travelers and crusaders who described the glories of Jerusalem after long years of wandering the Near East.

But those medieval wanderers faced a troublesome dilemma. None of them, or anyone they knew, had actually seen the object of their desire. In fact, for all they knew, there might not even be such a thing as this Holy Grail. They were searching for something that they had only seen in their dreams.

Such is the case with many of today's missionaries. Most have never seen anything that could even remotely be called an indigenous church. And so, among these valiant souls there are few of us who actually know what it is we are looking for.

Oh, but we think we know. Most pilgrims enter their journey already possessing a complete system of maps leading to the object of their quest. We have taken the right seminary courses and read all the right books. We have memorized the Three Selfs and the Ten Universal Principles—but something still eludes us.

In spite of our study, we somehow missed the bits and pieces that kept turning up along the way. If we had pieced these little scraps together they would have created a living mosaic, which seen from a distance, would have revealed to us the body of Christ in a new culture.

Sometimes we have missed the way because there was no one from whom to ask directions. Other times we have been too proud and sure of ourselves to seek out advice from the ones who would know. Either way, the results have been the same: Far too many pilgrims stopping at the more familiar places on the road rather than pressing on to the goal of their journey.

Like homesick travelers, many missionaries yearn for the trappings of their church culture back home— anything to feel comfortable. In time, this longing becomes so strong that any tradition offering a small taste of home becomes a strong lure. We stop, intending only to spend the night, but for many a weary and lost pilgrim the stay lasts a lifetime. Living in such comfortable places is much more secure than taking the risk to push out to where our goal might be found.

But the purpose of this pilgrimage is too important for us to allow our fellow pilgrims to stop at deceptive destinations. What if we can truly find this thing we are seeking? What if real, indigenous churches can be planted in new places?

These churches would then be sown in vast numbers, and we would expect that most of them would survive. These churches would require little care because they would be native. They would be fruitful because they would be indigenous. Rooted in time-honored rhythms of life and grounded in their own culture, they would *belong*.

If this ever happened, it would be the very thing the prophet Isaiah saw so long ago:

> *the glory of the Lord will fill the earth*
> *as the waters cover the beds of the seas.*

So much is at stake that it behooves pilgrims to help one another. Otherwise our journey ceases to be a stream of visionary men and women and becomes no more than a hapless lot of confused, weary people who are simply struggling to survive.

Those who have made good headway toward the goal, or those who have made any headway at all, must pass along the maps and markers that helped them find their way. Moreover, those who have not must be willing to receive them. This trail is no place for the fine, tailored robes of religious pride.

This is not to say that anyone, myself included, is anything close to an expert. Yet some pilgrims, by the grace of God, have been nearer to the goal than others. Some have seen it from afar and rejoiced.

This book is not a theological study of the concept of the indigenous church, nor is it a handbook for planting such churches. I am not qualified to write either. What I offer here is something closer to a journal—a collection of personal maps and markers written down by one pilgrim to pass on to another.

If you have dreams of seeing Christ draw His bride from some new people group, tribe, or tongue, then we are on the same pilgrimage. May what follows be of help, from the hand of one pilgrim to another, as we travel along this road together.

CHAPTER ONE

Land of the Steppe

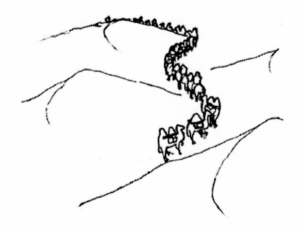

$\mathcal{T}$he following sketches from my own pilgrimage would be useless to fellow travelers without my first giving a picture of the territory through which we will roam. The twists and turns along the way would otherwise appear meaningless. With this in mind, I will begin by painting, in a few broad strokes, a portrait of the land in which we will journey together. It should help illuminate the insights that follow.

Yet it is difficult to write a concise description of Central Asia, this land of oasis and steppe, desert and mountain. About the size of the Australian sub-continent, Central Asia is a place of immense proportions. The steppe stretches for endless miles, while mountain peaks of over 20,000 feet seem to rise unexpectedly out of great deserts. Its incredible beauty almost defies words.

Also, the precise location of Central Asia is difficult to describe because the borders drawn by the natural forces of geography and kinship are more powerful than those of political will. This is something empire builders have learned the hard way, and something the thoughtful pilgrim should never forget.

A politician might say that post-Soviet Central Asia is the territory bordered by Russia on the north, Iran and Afghanistan on the south, the Caspian Sea on the west, and China on the east. But it is more realistic to draw Central Asia as that great expanse contained by Siberian plains in the north and the Hindu Kush mountains in the south. It starts as waves lap the shores of the oil rich Caspian Sea in the west, and ends somewhere in the measureless Taklamakan Desert to the east. This region is much more than a "post-Soviet province." It has always spilled over the lines of the best cartographers.

It could be that the term "post-Soviet" conjures up all manner of political questions in the minds of some pilgrims, questions that I will not address. As historians can testify, the affairs of state in this part of the world have always been fluid. Small kingdoms have fallen to great empires, which in turn give way to petty principalities, warlords, and semi-independent nations. In fact, political realities in Central Asia shift so often that to spell out them could make a fool out of me, for anything I write may change by the time you read this book.

However, our concern on this journey is not about geography or politics; as pilgrims, these neither obstruct us nor hold our allegiance. For our hearts are fixed upon something else—the region's millions who follow The Prophet.

Over ninety percent of Central Asians claim to follow Islam today, but this was not always the case. For centuries, the inhabitants of these lands were not Muslims. They were animists, believing that creatures, objects, and natural phenomena are inhabited by a myriad of spirits, each of which must be worshiped or appeased.

Before Islam, this primitive religion was challenged by more organized ones from the outside world. Buddhism, Zoroastrianism, and Nestorian Christianity all came trading their wares on the great Silk Road, but none has had the enduring impact of Islam, which has shaped the substance of life everywhere it has spread. Today it is almost impossible to imagine a Central Asia that is not dominated by Islam, but without such an imagination, we would make very poor pilgrims indeed!

While Islam's footprint has been long lasting it has never been deep, for the ancient darkness and fear of animism never completely gave way, its roots still spreading beneath the surface of Central Asian life. This is another point the wise pilgrim will do well to remember. So deep, so pervasive, are these roots that even the powerful religion of Mohammed was forced to adapt. This it did well, partly because of the way it entered the narrative.

Fittingly, Islam came to Central Asia riding with a caravan. Eager Arab traders from the west first opened the ancient Silk Road as a means to exploit the riches of the Far East; spreading their religion was a secondary consideration. Yet the almost military cadence of life in Islam appealed to the mercenaries whom the traders hired to guard their caravans, and the legendary Muslim honesty spoke volumes to the people in the bazaars.

But most of these traders were not trained in the strict ways of Islam's Shahari law. They were often simple men following a religion they barely understood themselves. From the beginning, Islam in Central Asia has not been overly complicated.

Even before the advance of mighty Muslim armies in the eighth century, the die was cast for Central Asia's future when the Arab trade caravans began carrying an influential new cargo—Islam's mystical pilgrims, the Sufi.

The Sufi were an odd lot, as hard to describe as modern pilgrims can be. They lived life as one continuous, spiritual journey, though unfortunately to the wrong destination. The religion they passed along was more mystical than legal, focused on spiritual experiences and not religious regulations. It is easy to understand why the region became, for the Sufi, a fruitful field. In their mystical message, the animist psyche of Central Asia had found a soul-mate.

The Muslim thrust into Central Asia was so successful that one eighteenth century Russian historian called it "the most solidly Islamic region of the world."

But our primary concern is not about geography or history; this pilgrimage is about matters alive and recent. So perhaps it is time to leave the past behind, gather our bags, and enter into the journey ourselves.

CHAPTER TWO

Point of Entry

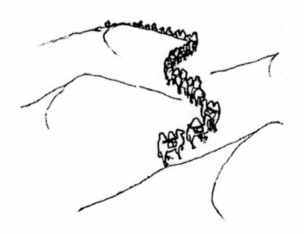

*W*hen someone departs on a trip, especially if it is going to be a long one, a crowd of well-wishers gathers at the railway station or airport. Tears flow as goodbyes are said, and promises to stay in touch are made by both parties. Most of us have been part of this scene at one time or another, so it is tempting to depict the start of our pilgrimage in these familiar terms.

However, trips have distinct starting places, points from which you depart. The kind of pilgrimage that we are joining really does not. It is something that must be entered. Like diving into a fast-moving stream, the pilgrim quickly senses a living history that was flowing before their arrival and that will continue after they are long gone.

When entering this pilgrimage, this search for a piece of God's heart, we join something bigger than ourselves. We have joined others in their devotion to a cause. We will slowly become bound together through the joys and hardships of the journey. In some miraculous way, we are entering into a human flow, for such a pilgrimage is not an individualistic affair. It is a communal event.

Community had hardly been a part of my vocabulary as a typical American. I had always been comfortable living my life as an individual, making my own decisions and pursuing my own goals. Like most of the men around me, I prided myself in being individualistic and self-sufficient. I assumed this journey would be the same. It seemed to me as if this was a part of the missionary ethos, to be the kind of person who can leave homeland behind and strike out alone.

However, I was soon to learn that my ideas and American ways were out of touch with the reality of life in Central Asia. I could not separate myself from those walking the trail alongside me, or from the footprints of those who have gone before. As this realization dawned on me, I was brought closer to the goal of our journey, for as we will discover later, indigenous churches are also communities. They are communities in ways that most of us have never really experienced in the West.

But we must not linger long in the realm of theory. I believe I hear the camels stirring.

The Sound of Being Foreign

It was a typical Friday afternoon in February. I had walked to the mosque beneath an overcast sky, with the temperature well below freezing. In the past, my trips to this brightly colored mosque had produced some incredibly focused times of spiritual warfare. Today my visit would produce something different.

Usually I could find a quiet spot to kneel in the back of the large hall, an inconspicuous place from where I could intercede for the souls of the men around me, who were devoutly following their prescribed acts of worship. Today, however, I had arrived at the mosque a little later than usual. The inside, nicely warmed, was packed wall-to-wall with bodies and I was forced retreat to the large porch. There the wind and the snow fiercely bit at my face.

I almost left. Inside I felt a strange, deep-seated resistance to being out in the open. I did not want to be out on that porch where I was exposed, and much more aware of my exposure. The shiver that traveled down my spine was caused by something more intimidating than the howling wind.

I tucked myself almost under a set of stairs, hoping that no one would notice that I was not participating in the Islamic prayers. As I settled in this quiet spot, I hoped that I would blend in. I received some puzzled looks as men shuffled by, but thankfully, most of them had other things on their minds—perhaps frostbite. None of them paid much attention to me.

For this I was glad. I was trying hard to go unnoticed while they were offering their prayers, for I knew that to be seen was to be found out. To be seen was to announce to them all that I did not belong.

As the speakers crackled and the wind blew light snow around our heads, the few hundred men began their worship. With military-like cadence, they went through the physical motions that correspond with Islamic prayers: turning the head to the right and left to acknowledge the angels supposed to be on either side; cupping the hands to the ears, which symbolizes listening to Allah; and bowing prostrate on the ground to show submission.

Each time the assembly of men dropped to their knees, the massive floor timbers shook from the force of their unity. And as they did, an unspoken message seemed to telegraph through my body and into my heart. I felt discordant, totally out of place. That, in turn, sent tiny signals out to the hairs on the back of my neck, something we normally call fear.

I am not sure why that day was any different; the routine had not changed. But this time I could almost hear it in the creaking floor joists and the crackle of the old loudspeakers. Deep inside it resonated repeatedly, "You are different. You do not belong. You are all alone."

Then it struck me. For one brief moment, in the slightest of ways, I understood what it must feel like to come out of Islam and follow Isa as Messiah and Savior. For a fleeting moment I had the incredible sensation of being out of sync with everyone else around me.

For my new brothers and sisters in Christ, this feeling is a daily part of their lives. All of Central Asia, their whole world, is moving in unison. At times they must feel hopelessly out of its rhythm. Most of them probably go through life desperately trying to hide in some corner, praying and hoping that no one notices them, just as I did that cold February afternoon.

Kneeling on those well-worn carpets I had heard the sound of being foreign. It could have shown me how little I understood what it means to be a Central Asian follower of Isa. I could have realized that I would never face the pressures they encounter when they embrace

Christ. I could have recognized that I would never experience the deep sense of pain that comes from living out of sync with one's own community.

I should have learned a lot that day, but the truth is that I didn't. At least, not for a long time. It was only in the following years that hindsight made these things clear. It had been an important moment in my journey; too bad I did not see it at the time.

Still, on that blustery Friday, God sowed in this pilgrim heart the seeds of truly indigenous thinking. They took a long time to bear fruit—perhaps I am more hard-headed than others—but something inside had begun to change.

Costly Advice

The apricot trees outside were in full bloom and the afternoon was awash in countless cups of tea, many more than I would have wanted. But I was doing what is expected of a guest in Central Asia and giving my host temporary control of my life. We were sitting on floor cushions around a low table with a carpet hanging on the whitewashed mud wall behind me. My gracious host with the bottomless teapot was a schoolteacher, a former Muslim who was now a follower of Isa. He also happened to be one of the most respected church leaders in the region.

It was because of my high regard for Muktar that I had traveled four or five hours for this visit. I wanted his advice on a list of important matters. However, it was not until later that I would learn the price to be paid for his wisdom.

After the effort it had taken to get there, I wanted to keep this particular meeting on track. Being a linear thinker, I feel good when a meeting goes according to my plan and become impatient and restless when I'm unsure of where the conversation is going.

As the afternoon wore on, I started feeling adrift. I could not bring the meeting into focus; in fact, it was starting to feel less like a meeting and more like a chat over a pot of tea. I couldn't even nudge us toward the first item on my agenda. The longer we talked, the harder I tried to turn our conversation to things more important—at least, important as I counted them.

After hours of frustrating small talk, the conversation finally took an encouraging turn. As he poured me yet another cup, Muktar looked me in the eyes and said, "You know, I like your ministry methods."

Like a sunbeam on a gray, rainy afternoon, his words warmed my soul. A mild sense of frustration had been simmering within me because of my neglected list. Now in its place sprouted a tiny blade of self-satisfaction as I contemplated these ministry methods of mine.

> *Pride goes before destruction,*
> *a haughty spirit before a fall.*

Before I could start to gloat, Muktar continued. "You came to see me without a plan, and that's the right way to do things in our culture. When someone comes to me with a list of things to discuss, they show that I'm only their 'business,' a project to be done. But ministry is not business, it is all about relationships."

His simple words, intended as a compliment, caught me unaware, like the suddenness of a sandstorm in the desert. One moment everything is fine and you can see to the horizon; the next you can't tell where you are.

In a sense I already knew this. After all, I had been a pastor in what seems like a previous life and I am very much a people person. Nonetheless, as a product of my culture, I still placed a high value on schedules, plans, lists, and agendas. These things are measurable. These things are valuable. Although I would never have admitted it to anyone else, these things proved to the world I was busy, and as a busy person I was *important.* At least, that's the way things had been counted back home in my world. But I was no longer in my world; I was now in his world, in Central Asia.

By his words and by his actions, Muktar was telling me that people and relationships take precedence over my beloved lists and agendas in this strange place he calls home.

Despite the fact that I had been living in Central Asia for two or three years, I had somehow avoided truly entering his world. I had managed to live in a façade, built to perfectly match my comfort zone. Now Muktar's kindly spoken words had shattered that illusion and startled me into reality.

Without knowing it, my friend had shaken my internal compass and now I could not find my bearings. One moment I was reveling in my good ministry methods, the next one much of my worldview was lost in a swirling confusion.

Muktar progressed to other topics, but I was stuck. The suddenness of it all had left me struggling. Part of me rejected what he had said, as it was just too hard to process. But another part hungered to see the world the way Muktar did, to reorient my compass to his North Star.

The rest of the afternoon was a blur. I do not remember anything else we talked about. As my host kept the time-honored rhythm with his teapot, I fought with an internal reality shift.

His words had struck a deep, uncomfortable chord within me. I could not even begin to concentrate on the rest of the conversation. The questions taking shape in my heart were almost audible.

"Will I really hear what he has to say?"

"How much am I willing to pay for the wisdom that will come from listening to this man?"

Somehow I knew that the answers would be expensive to me personally, perhaps costing more than I was willing to pay. It wasn't until much later that I remembered the words of a wise man who once said,

> *Though it cost you all you have,*
> *get understanding.*

When counting the cost for overseas missionary service, no one had told me that it might include a severely bruised ego.

My benign friend had not intentionally assaulted my self-esteem, and I know he wasn't being slyly sarcastic. That trait is neither in his personality nor in his culture. Muktar simply hadn't seen my mental agenda or the list in my coat pocket.

What I experienced that day was just one example of how a pilgrim is often required to purchase costly advice. But the expense is justifiable, for little by little such insights will shape our journey.

As a Western missionary who was addicted to his schedule, I had started out my pilgrimage with lists and agendas that seemed important. So important, in fact, that I almost trashed an invaluable friendship for their sake.

But for the grace of God, I might have communicated to this dear man that the cost of learning from him was too high for busy, important pilgrims like me.

CHAPTER THREE

Shrines

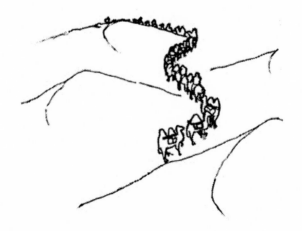

*A*nyone who has lived in Central Asia will find it hard to imagine the region without picturing a shrine. Shrines seem to be everywhere, sometimes built over important graves, but often only a lone tree holding ground on some isolated crag. The animistic soul of Central Asia cries out for a location to venerate, a place that will stand out as distinctly different from everything else. A place you can call holy.

Over the years, dirt trails become packed and stone ledges turn into polished stairways under the countless footfalls of barren women, crippled children, or other needy pilgrims searching for the supernatural. Eventually bricks are laid, and beautiful blue domes are erected. Thus is a shrine built.

However, it is not only the Muslim or the animist who desires a shrine. We Christians have shrines as well. Apart from the well-known official ones like the Via Dolorosa in Jerusalem and the Church of the Nativity in

Bethlehem, there seems to be a plethora of unofficial places that Christians are drawn to venerate.

Whether one travels to Bethlehem, Brownsville, or Toronto, it seems that all shrines are basically the same. They are simply places where people expect to find some kind of holy experience. Yet as soon as such a place becomes popular, what began as a search for communion with the Holy One becomes an institution. We build a roof over it, set a schedule of services, then count and record the numbers of visitors.

At best, shrines represent a convenient way to put God in a box. At worst, they become cheap magic. Just go to the right place, arrange for the right spiritual experience, and you will get your needs met. It's that simple.

Shrines also have a tendency to quickly become larger than life. Perhaps something miraculous happened there long ago, perhaps not. Who knows now? After a while that matters little, for the shrine has taken on a life of its own. The location becomes more important than the One who supposedly visited the common and made it un-common, and usurps the honor due to the One who came near and made it holy. Still, people continue to build shrines; Muslims, animists, and Christians. Even pilgrims have been known to do so.

But that is enough time spent here. We really should keep moving and find a place for the night. I fear a chill in the air.

A Shrine for Whom?

With hundreds in attendance, this was one of the largest gatherings of Central Asian Christians in recent memory. As one who had helped plan it, I glowed with fatherly pride. It was quite a show, but more than that, this was the indigenous church on display. Or so I would have said.

The worship music was played by some of Central Asia's finest musicians, Christians all of them. An ensemble of dancers in exquisite traditional costumes filled the platform, moving with choreographed precision. Just seeing their performance helped thaw January's cold. The spiritual fervor inside the hall made me feel close to the object of my journey.

I am certain that most people in the hall were duly impressed with the performance. I know we missionaries were. The whole evening was a well-polished stairway—

for us. How many times had I personally climbed it in the past? Here we had used a proven formula to leave the common outside, and create a warm, holy place inside. A glorious shrine, but built for whom?

Unfortunately, somewhere in the crowd there was at least one man who wasn't riding a spiritual high like the rest of us were by the end of the evening. The sad thing is, that man was a dear friend of mine.

Saeed was perhaps the most respected church leader in the region. At that time he had been a believer for about five years, which was longer than most of his compatriots. Furthermore, he was a tested man. From the beginning, from when he first turned to the light, he had been the leader of a church in his city. He had lived with troubles inside the church, and seemingly unending pressures from outside. He was a quiet man of proven spiritual reserves.

After driving six hours in mind-numbing weather, I doubt Saeed noticed the neat box we had built. Although they were only recent imports, Western church customs were quickly hardening like an oft-traveled pathway. As all good shrine builders before us, this evening represented our best efforts to manage and control the One who fills the universe.

Cold and weary, Saeed quickly spotted something that warmed him through to the heart. Up near the front of the crowd was an old, time-weathered Muslim man. Dressed in a costume sewn before most in the room were born, he personified tradition. His long white beard spoke of wisdom, respect, and of their shared Islamic heritage. Sitting ramrod straight in a wooden chair, he embodied the heart of this people. Saeed hoped that the old man represented something even more that night—a prophecy of the harvest to come.

Seated in all his proud tradition, the ancient visitor had come willing to listen, and tonight he would hear the gospel presented clearly—from another Central Asian. He would see hundreds of former Muslims openly worship Isa as their Savior, and hopefully, he would be moved to join them before the night was over. What better time could there be for a man near the end of his life to accept Christ?

Sadly it did not happen. In retrospect, I can see why.

The message was in the old man's language, but its style of logic and presentation was straight out of Dallas or Chicago. The words to the songs that evening were in his mother tongue, but they hardly sounded like his music. How could they, when they were mostly choruses translated from English?

I doubt that much of the program made sense to the old man whose wisdom came from living his whole life in Central Asia. Although I didn't realize it at the time, it became crystal clear to Saeed as the evening wore on. He realized that if he would ever *really* reach his own people, someone like that old man would need to find the gospel message much more attune to his world, not vice versa.

And what about the old man? I fear the evening only confirmed his worst fears. He had obviously come with an open mind, but I can almost hear him thinking halfway through the evening, "This message about Isa the Messiah is something foreign. Their worship is so strange, their ways so against everything our culture holds dear."

Of course that is conjecture. None of us actually knows what our old visitor thought that night. Before anyone could ask him, he quietly walked out of the shrine we had built to our church traditions and into a snowy Central Asian night.

I cannot say for sure what he thought as he went home, but I do know this. Very little the old man saw that evening would have made him feel like he belonged. There was none of the drama from his own culture. No greeting of the aged and respected. No telling of jokes. No eating together. And not a single cup of tea was served!

Granted, it is difficult to do those things in a meeting of three or four hundred people, and perhaps that's why Central Asians only occasionally hold such gatherings. We could have at least acknowledged the elders in the room and found place for a joke or two in the program. But no, like most other shrine builders, we had built what was comfortable for us.

In retrospect, I am afraid that we missionaries had unwittingly, yet perfectly, crafted a meeting to suit our own spiritual needs. Too little thought had gone into the spiritual needs of the hundreds of former Muslims and their kin whom we had invited to attend. What is worse, we had sent a clear message to the Central Asian believers in attendance that to be spiritual they must copy our church traditions. All the evening's familiar spiritual trappings had only taken us farther from the true object of our journey.

The combined effect of the evening had certainly produced a holy and moving experience, a shrine if you will. But whose heart was moved? Obviously not that of the old Muslim man who had slipped away early.

An indigenous church, by definition, will be strange and unfamiliar to foreign missionaries. In fact, it is often the things that we pilgrims do not like or understand that make something truly indigenous. The well-worn ways of one culture can never speak into the heart of another.

The Western culture has many convenient ways to produce just the right spiritual experiences for those from it—a multitude of neat boxes to keep God manageable. I don't think many of us had even considered that our magic, which never failed to charm us, might not have the same effect on our Central Asian friends.

CHAPTER FOUR

Caravansary

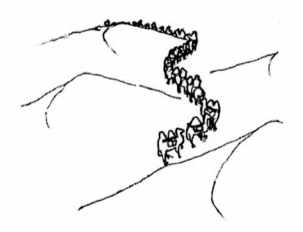

$\mathcal{T}$ he word *caravan* paints a familiar picture—a convoy of camels or donkeys and a group of travelers, all banded together for protection. These have been common across Asia since time immemorial.

The second part of the word is trickier. The term *sary* is used throughout Central Asia, especially out in the countryside. It means either *guest room* or *barn*. A strange mixture of ideas, but quite accurate. Caravansaries were frontier outposts along the trade routes, exotic places visited by all kinds of characters— serious-faced military men, petty thieves, even an occasional Magi traveling from the east. The caravansary combined the features of a hotel and restaurant with a military post, and of course, a bazaar.

These little stopping places often begin as no more than a clear little spring. Such waters are delightfully refreshing places in dry, desolate Central Asia. Then, as word gets out, it becomes a popular place for weary travelers to stop and rest. More pilgrims hear about this pleasant little spring of water, a comfortable place to stop for a bit and be refreshed from the difficulties of the road. Maybe they decide to spend the night, maybe stay just a little while longer.

In no time at all, what was no more than a wide spot in the road is transformed into an oasis of rest. A few amenities from home make this dusty stopping place seem like a palace to the weary pilgrim. The caravansary soon becomes part of the tales that are told when traders, pilgrims, and other travelers return home.

Though, as more travelers come, someone must accommodate the increase. Eventually one brave soul is asked to stay around for a while to help others negotiate the strange environment, and maybe organize just a bit.

Usually the one asked to stay is a gifted administrator. As he operates in his gift, others see the great value of his service. His work makes the way smoother for others who would like to enjoy the spring. This in turn causes even more to visit. Of course, for the one with an administrative gift, all this activity brings a deep sense of personal and professional satisfaction.

Without anyone realizing it, a caravansary has been built. What had once been a remote little spring has now become a hub of activity, with traders and pilgrims constantly coming and going. But what is wrong with that? The more, the better, right?

Yet as they come, a whole new set of *needs* develop—the *need* for some kind of structure, the *need* for administration. With so many visitors, needs arise faster than the midday sun on the Steppe.

Visitors *need* places to eat and drink—thus restaurants are opened.

They *need* places to sleep—thus rooms are built.

Their pack animals *need* a place out of the weather— thus barns are erected.

Without a doubt, the development of the caravansary was certainly *need-driven*, but from where did all this need come? Did the simple little spring really need all this organization to continue giving water? Will it be able to *continue to give* its clean, clear water surrounded with all this structure?

Several years ago I stumbled across the remains of an old caravansary while driving out to visit some friends. It is one of seven in that region, so they tell me, which fortified the borderlands between the Russian and Chinese empires. It has become my favorite place to stop and rest whenever I travel on that road, the shade of its ancient trees providing a welcome break after five hours behind the wheel. But other than the trees, there is not much left—some old mud walls and a few traces of the buildings that once stood inside their enclosure. Still, there is something magical about the place. It is exciting just knowing that it was once so vibrant and full of life.

Perhaps everyone sooner or later discovers their own broken, empty hull of a caravansary. Maybe it is just part of the journey?

Too Many Pilgrims

Not all that long ago, a group of missionaries from a number of different countries came together to plant a church. Not just any church, mind you. They wanted to plant a truly indigenous church in the most strongly Islamic quarter of a certain large Central Asian city. They desired to see a church started in the same neighborhood as one of the most famous mosques in the land. This was a bold step of faith.

This unusual team, including former Muslims from a nearby country, spent hours on their knees, asking God to pour out His mercy on this neighborhood. They walked its streets in expectation that the Holy Spirit would, at any moment, lead them to people who were good soil for the Word of God.

And in a remarkably short period, it happened! In a matter of just months, these bold pilgrims saw their vision birthed. A small band of new believers worshiping Isa in their homes had emerged within earshot of the call to prayer from the most famous mosque in all the land! Something splendid was happening here.

These new brothers and sisters were all from Muslim families, so they knew very little about the Bible. They had much to learn. Yet each time this little flock gathered, they were a living testament to the power of God's Spirit to work even in hardened places.

This young church was so successful that word began to spread. The missionaries involved wrote home to their organizations and friends. They were excited to tell about what God had done in a difficult place.

Soon some mission leaders decided that this was something they should see. When they arrived, these wise leaders were duly impressed with what they saw. They understood that what they were seeing was something truly indigenous. It was therefore decided that this would be the ideal place for some future missionaries, and maybe a few key financial supporters, to gain exposure to the workings of a "real" indigenous church.

Soon the first small group arrived, then another one or two. Each group was greatly encouraged by what they saw. For many this was the first time they had encountered a church that did not pattern itself on the West. Plans were quickly laid for a few more groups to visit—just a few at first, but ever so slowly, the numbers of these short-term pilgrims increased. As they did, there arose a whole new set of *needs* to be met.

Visitors *need* a place to which they can emotionally connect—thus a building is purchased.

They *need* decent places to sleep—thus rooms are built.

They *need* comfortable transportation—thus vans are bought.

And so on. And so on.

When it comes to pilgrims, it seems that *needs* arise faster than the midday sun on the Steppe.

Without anyone noticing it, and in short order, a perfect little caravansary had been constructed. The whole thing was need-driven, but no one asked the vital question, "Just exactly *whose* needs are driving all this?"

In no time at all, the place had become a hub of activity, with mission leaders and other short-term pilgrims coming and going on a regular basis. But what is wrong with that? The more, the better, right?

After a few years, some of the original missionaries took time to sit back and reflect. So much good had happened in such a short period. Or so it had seemed at first. A multitude of short-term visitors had come, served, and then returned home with vision. Is that not something to be proud of?

But there is a catch. As these pilgrims passed through, the clear little spring they visited was trampled. In fact, it had been altered beyond recognition. In its place there was now a great deal of structure and administration—a well-run caravansary, but very little indigenous church.

In order to accommodate the missionaries and their foreign guests, the group of new believers had to constantly adapt to the needs of outsiders. But the more they adapted, the less of an indigenous a church they became.

With every new group of pilgrims who came *to serve*, the needs that pressed upon the young church grew heavier. A multitude of quiet demands to yield ground met this simple group of indigenous believers, who could not possibly withstand such a barrage of guests and remain unchanged. The pressure was too great.

Slowly, and without anyone recognizing it, the needs of the pilgrim engulfed the needs of the indigenous church. In fact, so completely did one overwhelm the other, that I don't think anyone even noticed that the two were not the same.

The simple truth is that the needs that shape an indigenous church are often invisible to missionaries. The factors required for its survival are diametrically opposite to the needs of those on a pilgrim's journey.

We need exposure. They need protection and covering.

We need to impress the wealthy. They need to minister to the impoverished.

We need to gather large numbers in order to feel important. They need to gather in mere handfuls in order to risk intimacy and community.

Perhaps the question should have been asked: "Have we missionaries forgotten who came to serve whom?"

There it is. And as strange as it might sound, it is the truth. Yet it is such truth that often makes us uncomfortable. However, sometimes the pilgrim should spend a night out in the open. No caravansary. No shelter from harsh reality.

Perhaps it is the right time to ask ourselves why we spend so much time building structures when we could be building lives? Does the kingdom of God really need these structures or do we? Are we afraid that without caravansaries we will have no way to show the world what we have done, no proof that we are valuable?

[handwritten margin note: Collecting the Church]

[handwritten margin note: worthy motive?]

But in some ways this is a moot point, at least for that caravansary, for today there is no longer an indigenous church in the most strongly Islamic quarter of a certain big Central Asian city. Today there is not much left besides some nice little meetings attended by a handful of former Muslims who have become well-versed at serving the needs of the many pilgrims who are just passing through.

Yet it remains one of my favorite places. I mentally stop there whenever I can. There is something magical about the place. It is exciting just knowing that it was once so vibrant and full of life.

I hope none of my fellow pilgrims are forced to discover a broken down, empty caravansary of their own. It seems these things are always located much too close to the heart. But on the other hand, maybe it is just part of the journey? One might even say that it is good for a pilgrim to face his insecurities and fears surrounded by the crumbling walls of familiar structures, for this helps to clarify our vision about what the indigenous church is, and what it is not.

Furthermore, catching sight of this ruin might be enough to tell us that we have reached a very important moment. Most likely, we are now utterly lost.

CHAPTER FIVE

On Being Lost

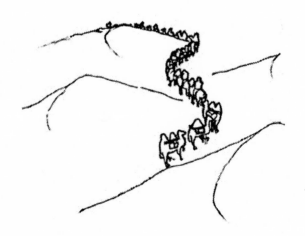

To admit that one is lost should not cause a great deal of shame, for it is nothing new. People have been losing their way for a long, long time. Listen to the words from an ancient book, written by a prophet named Moses:

> *Remember how the LORD your God led you*
> *all the way in the desert these forty years,*
> *to humble you and to test you*
> *in order to know what was in your heart.*

To the pilgrim who feels like they have been wandering in circles, I say take heart, you are not alone. It seems that we are in good company.

I know this might be of little consolation to most. As products of Western culture, we know that progress is the name of the game. Pilgrims and progress, they kind of go together.

The truth is, the crux of the pilgrim's experience is to *go* somewhere. It is bad to get stuck even for a short while. But to spend years without having made much headway would be akin to a prolonged death sentence. And unfortunately, this brutal punishment is not carried out in private. Rather it seems like many want to stand by and watch. Sometimes the pilgrim feels like a spectacle before the world.

Now you should know that the audience does not mean us any harm, but drifting about lost in front of a crowd can become unnerving, especially when it involves one particular group who watch our progress more closely than most. Let me explain.

Down through the years, the majority of pilgrims have not been independently wealthy. To overcome this embarrassing problem of cash flow, they have usually sought out wealthy patrons to help finance their holy journeys. And so it is with modern pilgrims; we likewise have our patrons. We call them by different names now, but not much else has changed.

I am referring to those generous people back home who give money to support our ministry, finance the budget, or whatever you call it. I mean the ones who we hope will keep on giving so our kids can eat.

However, as those on the receiving end of this deal, it is important that we realize the reason why these patrons give their hard-earned money. It is not just because they like us. Nor is it because they want our kids to grow into happy, well-adjusted adults. *conecction*

No. They give because they believe. They believe in the same things that we do. Their soul is stirred by the same visions that stir ours. As people of similar convictions, our patrons long to see what we have seen, to feel, even just touch, what we have felt. They watch our progress closely only so they might glimpse the journey through our eyes.

This is at once comforting and the source of many a midnight anxiety attack. Deep inside, most pilgrims have at one time or another asked themselves, "What will all these wonderful people think if they find out I am lost?"

Don't forget, our patrons love us. They really do believe in us. Most of them weep with us in our struggles and rejoice with us in our triumphs. Just knowing this brings comfort to the weary soul.

But there is something else that most of us also know. We understand perfectly well that our patrons have the legitimate desire to know that their money is being well spent. Like good accountants, they want to see

71

the numbers add up, in a spiritual sort of way. And why shouldn't they? Nevertheless, this knowledge strikes fear in the heart of one who is acutely aware of his own bankruptcy.

What kind of newsletter should pilgrims send home when they aren't making any progress? Just what do we say if we are feeling befuddled and confused? How can we even begin to tell our patrons that we have become lost along the way? Not "lost" in the theological sense of the word, but rather "lost" in the normal sense. Lost, like someone who took a wrong turn or two but is not sure where? Somewhere we missed the signs, and now we honestly don't know where we are, or even how to get back on track.

Most, if not all, pilgrims have found themselves at this point some time or another on their journey. It is an emotionally charged moment when residual fears from childhood intersect with the ones we have cultivated as adults, distorting our perspective and making it hard to find God. It is a place where the fear of rejection raises the specter of economic ruin, and failing at one small task escalates into the certainty of being a *failure*. It is a terrifying place, but it is also a shining moment of truth.

It is also, if I remember correctly, the exact point where the path splits into three roads, each leading to a very different destination. This lonely place, where each pilgrim comes face-to-face with some uncomfortable choices, is now before us.

The Left Path

After long and careful deliberations, some pilgrims veer to the left. It's a nice-looking trail—wide, smooth, and well-used. Those who choose to follow its course soon find themselves with a whole new language. They begin to speak "evangelistically," as some call it. Here's how it happens.

As someone who is still new to this pilgrimage thing, they try to describe the lands of their journey to their patrons back home. When they do, their audience is easily impressed by the images from this exotic new world. Then it so happens that the pilgrim receives a gushing response after having told some simple story, with a few extra details thrown in—by accident, of course.

In time, exaggerating a little here and enlarging a little there becomes the rule of thumb. Soon the journey's most insignificant moments are recast as exciting spiritual adventures or life-threatening perils. It is a fast downhill slide from there.

Just like learning any new language, fluency grows with use. Quicker than you can say "quagmire," what felt awkward in the beginning is now like our mother tongue. Once we start speaking "evangelistically" in our newsletters and sermons, people come to expect it. We are soon ensnared by our own words.

Back at the trailhead this seemed like a glorious, upward path, one well worth traveling on for years. But lately there have been rumors that it eventually leads down to one of Central Asia's great salt flats, known for their large poisonous vipers. With that said, may I suggest we search for a different route?

The Middle Path

The middle path is the obvious one for us to explore next. With only a quick glance, it becomes clear that it is going to be more difficult than the left path. It will require real work. Nevertheless, it is a very attractive option. In fact, it seems to be the path of choice based on the pilgrim traffic around us.

Thanks to the recent spread of technology, this middle choice has also become simpler than ever to follow. Make a quick run to the Xerox center downtown and presto! One can solve any ministry problem in this new land with the push of a button.

If someone is an experienced singer or song writer, they can quickly teach others to faithfully imitate the melodies that were so comfortable back home. If a pilgrim is even moderately talented in the performing art we call preaching, they can surely Xerox their act in many a Central Asian oasis.

No longer is there a need to struggle and strive to draw an original. The photocopy path does away with that difficult toil. Simply choose a favored version, which is usually that of our home church, make a few minor adjustments in the toner level, hit Print, and voila! Out comes a new indigenous church!

This trail has a couple of attractive benefits. First of all, the plans and preconceived ideas that we brought with us fit right in. For even though we might have traveled 14,000 miles and crossed 12 time zones, everything on this path is recognizable, even familiar. Everything is nice and orderly—in a Western sort of way—and we foreign pilgrims feel very much at home.

Second, this nice, neat church makes everyone happy. Everyone, that is, except for the Central Asian believers who are undergoing culture shock every Sunday morning.

Once they enter that sacred door they cross into an unreal world where spirituality is often equated with punctuality, even though they have known since childhood that nothing important ever starts on time. After a lifetime of sitting on warm floor cushions, they are obliged to position their bodies on cold metal chairs to meet with God.

Since this middle path is a popular route, perhaps I should explain in some detail how it is navigated. It is rather simple, so it is no small wonder that many choose this direction. I know it was easy for me, but I will save that story for later.

There are only three important steps in navigating the middle path:

1. Start with young people, those young enough that they are still compliant and won't question your authority. Be careful when dealing with mature adults, especially a grown man with a family. They have a tendency to mess up the best-laid plans.

2. Now throw in some money, but little by little, and not too much in one place. It doesn't matter what currency is used, but we have found that US dollars work best in Central Asia. With them, almost anything can be done—rent meeting halls, print literature, even buy loyalty.

3. The last of the three steps is certainly the most fun, for now we begin to accessorize our hard work with some colorful costumes and customs. Exotic hats and dances work great, and Central Asia has some of the finest.

Time has shown this to be a most successful route. Many a large church has been started on this path. Of course, it's a different question altogether to ask if any of them are actually indigenous.

In spite of its obvious attractions, a word of caution about this middle path may be in order here. There are a few small difficulties in store for the pilgrim who chooses this direction.

First, this middle course is not for those on a budget. It can become expensive to keep the new friends happy once we become their source of all good things. Our friends soon lose faith in us when we cannot live up to their expectations. Besides, real friendships are built on equality and reciprocity, things that do not develop when everything is a one-way street.

The second problem is that the young people chosen for leadership may be impressionable and easy to control, but they also have little authority in their community. Central Asian society has this bothersome habit of honoring the wisdom that comes from living a long time, raising a family, and having the grey hair to prove it.

This can truly become annoying if a few years down the road some of those young and easily controlled leaders grow into strong-willed adults. They may actually start expecting that *we* listen to *them*! This is a troubling role-reversal for the pilgrim who is accustomed to being in control.

Some might say that this particular path is shallow. And the truth is, this choice usually holds so little soil that it seldom grows anything that could be called indigenous. But it is not our place to judge such matters, and we do not have to. The harsh, inhospitable spiritual climate of Central Asia is more than capable of pronouncing its own verdict. For you see, the most discouraging part of this well-worn path is its destination. After years of hard work, pilgrims may find themselves somewhere other than where they had hoped. It makes for a most miserable morning when a pilgrim awakes to find himself at the wrong destination. I should know.

Personal Explorations in the Middle

It was hot and dry the morning I awoke at the wrong destination. Or should I say, it was very unpleasant the morning I awoke at the wrong destination and realized that it was wrong. I was standing among nice straight rows of folding chairs at church after a well-ordered Sunday morning worship service, enjoying a bit of small talk with a young woman I'll call Sofia.

Sofia was the fruit of a joint effort of sorts. Early in my journey I had partnered with a talented, hard-working fellow pilgrim. Together we dreamed of starting a training center where we would "train the future leaders of the indigenous church." As a slogan it sounded so good, so much like something from a missions textbook. Sofia was one of our first students; she was also one of our very few students, for God, in His mercy, did not allow our training center to last long.

Nevertheless, what I had seen this morning was proof that we could train good leaders at our training center. This former student of ours was bright and energetic. She could preach, teach, and pray with the best of them. She even spoke a little English. No doubt about it, she would go far.

Perhaps farther than I had thought.

This young and inexperienced lady had already become a key leader in an equally young and inexperienced church. Yet she and the church seemed to be doing quite well. Her performance thus far had made our training center proud. As befitting my role in her ministry's development, I decided to engage in some appropriate small talk after the service that morning.

"So, it seems God is blessing this little church of yours," I said in my most pastoral voice. I was not expecting a real reply; a little meaningless Christian jargon would have been fine. You know, the things we usually say to the pastor after a Sunday morning service. That is not what came in return.

Perhaps we had not schooled Sofia well in the subtle undertones of being religious, for her reply came straight from the heart. Like a flash flood in the desert, its muddy waters surged with raw, but honest, power.

"Do you really think this is *our* church?" she responded. "Do you see anything here that is *ours*?

Everything is imported from your world." Pointing around us Sofia continued: "This... this order... this structure... this is not my culture. If I ever go somewhere else, I want to act like the Apostle Paul, not like missionaries! Why couldn't you have come here and acted like an apostle?"

As fast as it had come, the flood of emotion was gone. In its place was a heavy sigh as Sofia concluded, "I used to want this to be our church, but now I'm too tired to keep trying. Missionaries brought us so much of their culture mixed with the gospel that it will never grow here."

What does one do at a moment like this? I personally have no idea. Should I even try to answer what was obviously not a question?

As Sofia walked away I stood there stunned. For several minutes I struggled with how to respond, even if only to myself. Much later I realized that this was when I had reached my own lonely moment of truth—that terrifying place where my childhood fears intersected with adult ones, where the specter of *failure* began to haunt the corners of my mind. Before me lay different roads on which to travel, each leading to very different destinations. Which road would I choose?

Over time, the disappointment and pain on Sofia's face would force me to deal with some very uncomfortable choices. The smugly self-righteous option would be to blame the missionary with whom she now worked. It is always easier to point the finger somewhere else, and this is exactly what we do when we are guilty to the bone and know it. But deep inside, I knew something else was wrong, something much more fundamental to my ministry, yet I was not sure if I had the strength of will to deal with it.

This is the way God will lead a pilgrim, and this is how I was brought to the third fork in my road.

The Unlikely Third Fork

This may be a good time to review exactly how we came to find ourselves here. Sometime back we waxed philosophical about the concept of being lost. Not just a little off-course, but hopelessly lost. The "walking circles in the desert" kind of lost. And just as that idea was starting to sink in, we stopped to consider the benevolent patrons back home who have helped us get this far. They are the ones who love us and believe in us, but they still need some kind of progress report if we want them to keep supporting us on this journey.

So in spite of our utter lost-ness, we realized the need to do *something*. This was the place where the road broke into three separate paths. This blinding moment of truth exposed our wretchedness and forced us to choose how we would deal with our condition.

We looked first to the left, finding a pathway strewn with simple tricks like speaking "evangelistically" or sensationalizing everyday events. Mercifully our corrupt nature was convicted by the Holy Spirit as we gazed longingly in that direction, so we turned the camels and headed away.

Then we saw the middle fork, a more inviting trail with its quick, Xerox copies. With only the most minor adjustments, we were able to import a complete church tradition from our home culture and transplant it into this foreign soil. We found we could cover much ground if we would but kidnap a few young people out of their culture and throw some money around. With amazing speed we would be able to produce something to show for our journey, something that would prove to ourselves, and to our patrons, that we are not lost after all.

Apart from speed, this trail has many advantages. The most noticeable are the series of orderly meetings that are certain to make most pilgrims happy. Unfortunately, the list of disadvantages is just as long. This is especially so for the bewildered local believers who cannot understand much of what goes on in their own church.

This particular path, the middle one as we have called it, is well traveled. Some pilgrims will spend a career pressing forward on this alluring trail. Of course, it should be remembered that others may have to spend *their* careers cleaning up the debris of the heartbreaks strewn along its way.

So now it seems that the path winding off to the right is the only one remaining for us to explore. I say explore because it is still mostly uncharted. Few there are who travel its way.

At first glance, this path is not attractive at all. In fact, one might say that it looks rather bleak. I doubt any of us will be sending home pictures from this part of the journey. But sometimes life leaves us with little choice. Even though the road ahead appears rigorous, I believe it is our best hope for the future. So just what is this last path?

It is an unpretentious little thing called the truth.

In order to travel along this path we simply write to our beloved patrons and tell them that we don't really know what we are doing. We must freely admit that we haven't yet seen what an indigenous church will look like here. And, unless someone shows us, we doubt that we ever will. This path requires us to stop leading others to believe that we are some kind of spiritual giants. We come clean with everyone—our friends, our family, our supporters, and our God.

By being honest we find that we can no longer take credit for any good thing that happens. All the credit, all the praise, will have to rise to Someone else. But in exchange for the applause of people we may just find something of greater value. Once we stop building shrines and caravansaries for ourselves, we will be able to see wonderful signs up ahead.

CHAPTER SIX

Signs in the Sky

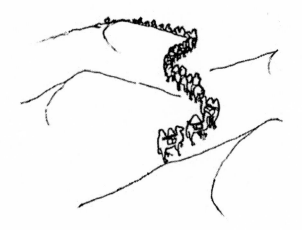

T he deserts of Central Asia are vast. Some are sand and dunes, others simply rock and dust—mile after endless mile of lung-choking dust. The best way to describe them is by using the Russian word for them, *pustinya*, which means "empty" or "nothing-ness." These are places of nothing—great, howling, empty places.

This vast barrenness that covers over sixty percent of Central Asia's topography is not confined to the physical; it is often characteristic of the spiritual landscape as well. The pilgrim wandering in Central Asia will often stagger through such places, frequently and easily becoming lost.

Imagine passing through such a fearsome place. Then remember that this is a journey for which there is no map, and one for which you have no clear idea of what your destination actually looks like. If that image sends a shiver down your spine, perhaps you will feel sympathy toward the failures and mistakes of pilgrims like myself, who have often been lost in this spiritual wasteland.

"Beat the crowds! Sign up now for the next outbound caravan leading into the great and never-ending wastelands!" Doesn't sound too appealing, does it?

The terrifying image of being hopelessly lost in a trackless waste will help us appreciate the fact that pilgrims need something to point the way. If we could but find such a marker, it would be worth all our worldly possessions—including the trinkets and traditions that we brought from home.

Or imagine a motley band of tired, thirsty pilgrims wandering through this same desert. Although they set out on this journey full of hope and promise, they are now hopelessly lost, and desperate for a sign.

As the sun sinks below a dune, they see something bewildering. At first it appears to be an odd, second sunset. Could it be another mirage, of which they have seen many? Yet as the darkness slowly envelops them, it becomes clear that whatever this thing may be, it is certainly real. Eerily it hangs as a sign in the night sky, its glowing light beckoning all to follow. This strange

Illustration

heavenly sign breathes new hope into the lost pilgrim. Perhaps, *just perhaps*, there is a way out of this wasteland.

In times past, pilgrims, traders, and caravan owners along the old Silk Road relied on a specialized navigation system that was perfected just for them—the fire tower. These great edifices were constructed at the command and kindness of various local sovereigns whose cities sat on the major caravan routes.

These ancient signs, the fire towers, were built of strong, sun-baked bricks so they could reach into the sky. The idea was to thrust great torches high enough so that their light could be used as a point of navigation in the featureless desert.

An ornate brick example is still standing today in the ancient caravan city of Bukhara in Uzbekistan. For a few pennies the adventuresome pilgrim can climb the winding inner staircase to the parapet where the Muzzem stands five times a day to call Muslims for prayer. Its elegant silhouette rises over 150 feet, having been one of the tallest structures in the world when it was built in 1127 AD. It was said that at night, the fire tower of Bukhara could be seen for hundreds of miles!

Unknown to us at the beginning of this magnificent journey, a great and benevolent Sovereign had already raised up certain fire towers along our route. For some reason, it is important to Him that we are able to find the way. These blazing signs that He has placed can help us find the way to the object of our pilgrimage even under the worst of conditions. And what conditions could be worse for a pilgrim than deeply-engrained cultural arrogance and spiritual pride?

Because of their imposing stature, you may think these impressive torches in the night sky would be obvious to any traveler—but this is not always the case. Sometimes it can be hard to see things that we *don't want to see.*

Perhaps it would be best if I describe, in detail, some of the fire towers I have found along the way. This pilgrim is deeply indebted to these signs and wants to spare others the agony of seeing them only in retrospect, as he often did.

CHAPTER SEVEN

A Late Night Challenge

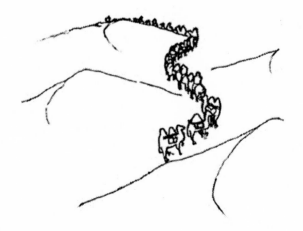

I suppose you could say that I had reached a personal milestone. I was now certain that I knew absolutely nothing about the indigenous church. At least, not what it should look like in Central Asia. It was completely beyond me. I was forced to admit that I had yet to see anything that could honestly be classified as indigenous. And worst of all, I did not even know where to look.

It may be difficult for some to appreciate what a loathsome place this was, but try to envision it. I had spent great sums of other people's money. My family and I had traveled halfway around the world so that I could be the "expert," that is, the missionary. Instead, I was compelled to admit that I knew nothing. Zilch. This was a humiliating moment of self-awareness, which I would have gladly kept all to myself had it not been for writing this book.

Around the same time something else came into view. It started out small and troubling to see, but in time, it grew to become a great fire tower. Torches blazing into the sky, its light completely revealed my ignorance. Thankfully, it also illuminated something of much greater importance. By its light I began to see who it was that would know what an indigenous church should look like.

This heavenly sign first came into view when I visited some friends. Akim Jan and his wife Rena were going through hard times. Their difficulties were probably the same as those of any who would dare to pioneer a church among their own people. It is hard work to shepherd precious souls as they are fleeing Islam to find refuge in Isa as their tower of deliverance. Akim Jan and Rena were pouring out their lives in a difficult place under trying circumstances. For the most part their reward had been a slap in the face. They knew that their Master had warned that it would be this way, but this knowledge did not make things easier.

One beautiful spring day, shortly after the ice melted off the mountain pass, I went to see Akim Jan and Rena with the hope that I could give some good counsel, to somehow help them in their troubles. In time, however, I would realize that it was I who got the better end of the deal that day. In retrospect, I received much more valuable advice than I gave that night.

The evening wore on and late into the night, under a bare 40-watt bulb, I was still listening to these unpretentious servants of God pour out their disappointment and anger. Most of it came from the same things that hurt church leaders back home—gossip, unforgiveness, backbiting, and the like. As someone who has been in that position before, I could counsel them through this kind of pain. However, they also faced hurts that most pilgrims will never know. In addition to the normal church problems, they also had to cope with the sinful attitudes of missionaries.

Now rest assured, most missionaries I know are true saints. I really mean that. Few of them ever commit any *big* sins. But it is the inconspicuous little things such as spiritual pride that have caused many a missionary pilgrim to become hopelessly lost. I am referring to the kind of spiritual pride that develops during the years of study and preparation for missions. The kind that makes us slow to listen, but quick to give advice. This pride puffs the head up with knowledge even while the heart withers from a lack of grace. It is a devious enemy, especially hard to see when it is stuck in one's own eye.

But on this night, by the grace of God, someone began to remove the log from mine. The blindness began to clear as I heard my friends tell what they see when we missionaries indulge in this subtle sin. I heard of the pain we often cause the very people we say we love.

Normally, such a distasteful subject would never be allowed to come up with guests. Not in Central Asia, where hospitality and saving face are so important. However, in the course of conversation that evening, I could tell that there was something bothering my friend, but Akim Jan would not say what. So I probed.

"Something is bothering you Akim," I said. "What is it? You know we can talk about anything."

The look on his face told me I had hit a nerve, but true to his culture, he stonewalled me. So I gently pushed some more. After much prodding he finally said, "Oh, you really don't want to know."

My nerves were still frazzled and my body sore from the bone-jarring six-hour taxi ride to Akim Jan's house, and this quick, off-hand dismissal would not do. I pushed one more time insisting, "Yes I do. I really do want to know what you're thinking."

I have always heard that there is something in Central Asian culture about asking three times. I do not know if that was it, but the genie came out of the bottle. As Akim Jan began to speak, his tone was not cross and his expression was not angry. However, his words were uttered with the surety of a man who had given long thought to the subject at hand.

"Missionaries are often difficult to work with," he said. "They don't treat us with very much respect." He was referring to himself and his wife. "Sometimes they ask our opinion, but they don't really want to know what we think. They actually just want us to agree with their ideas and plans."

I listened intently as he continued. "And it is the same for all of us," he said, broadening the scope to include other Central Asian church leaders we both knew. "On a few occasions we have been honest and said what we really thought. But our opinion did not matter. The missionaries still did exactly what they wanted. They didn't listen to us."

Even before he was done speaking, I was contemplating my response. Of course this kind of thing happens from time to time, I thought. We're all human, brother.

In addition, I did not miss the polite way he used the third person, "the missionaries." I knew he was trying to be careful. But since I too am one of "the missionaries," I was somewhat offended. I *knew* I never acted this way.

Now that I had coaxed him out of his cultural norms, I decided that we should follow mine. Being an American, I am well-versed at using honesty as a bludgeon to silence dissent. As Christians we do it all the time—in the spirit of "speaking the truth in love," of course. So I proceeded to tell Akim Jan that even if some missionary had hurt him personally in the past, this was not the norm. Perchance there was some unforgiveness in his heart that he needed to deal with?

To tell you the truth, I was a bit disappointed in Akim Jan. He was normally very mature, and I thought him a very spiritual man. So why was he behaving so differently tonight?

He responded with the same surety as before, issuing me a simple challenge: "Check it out. Ask the others I mentioned. See what they say. *If* you can get them to speak openly about it with you."

The way his voice stressed the word *if* was a reminder that in Central Asian culture, honored friends are treated with utmost respect. It can be very hard to extract an honest opinion from a friend when they think it will hurt your feelings. Nevertheless, Akim Jan's challenge disturbed me enough that I still had to try. I was sure I would prove him wrong.

Many Questions, Painful Answers

So I started asking questions. Lots of questions. Over the next few months, I pushed. I probed. I probably embarrassed some of my Central Asian friends by my quest for the truth. In their worldview, some things are better left unsaid. But I pushed until it came out. Eventually even their cultural taboo against offending friends could not hide it. To my shame, I found out that Akim Jan was right. So right that it made me ill.

Every Central Asian leader with whom I spoke echoed his assessment. Oh, they were very polite and indirect about it. It is their culture. But in each case, after skirting around the issue, they all agreed that most missionaries do not want to know what local believers think. It is often irrelevant to us. When we want to do something, we just do it. Maybe it has something to do with the fact that we control all the resources?

This painful truth stung like a scorpion in my shoe—again and again. How could I get away from the indictment? How many times had I personally been guilty?

I started to realize that I usually value my own opinion much more than I honor the wisdom that comes from living one's whole life in Central Asia.

Furthermore, when I so casually discard the advice of these mature men of God, I project a lack of respect for them personally. *Ouch!*

So painful was the glimpse of this sign that something had to give. I could not really hear what they were saying and just keep doing ministry as usual. I had to either write it off as a mirage, or follow it as a sign from heaven. I chose the latter. My ideas about missions and ministry slowly began to change.

I realized I could push my own agenda by exploiting the tremendous respect I am given as a missionary, or I could draw on this respect and influence the ideas that arise indigenously. I could offer my years of experience and Bible training as a resource to local leadership, or I could use their gifts as a resource for myself. But I could not do both.

Until now I had actually missed the meaning of the word *indigenous.* I had failed to see that it means a way of thinking that I as a foreigner would never completely understand. So I started asking more questions than I answered. I started trusting local leaders more, and myself and other missionaries less.

When the trauma of having a log wrenched from my eye wore off, I started anxiously searching the horizon for other fire towers. I had found one extremely precious sign and did not want to miss any others that might continue to guide my journey.

Without a doubt, Akim Jan's late night challenge grew to be the most important point of navigation on my pilgrimage. It showed me many of the places where I had wandered lost. Its light cast long shadows on many of the things that I had previously been so sure of, and it pointed me in a new but unfamiliar direction.

Whereas in the past I thought I knew so much, now I had only questions. Lots of them. I simply did not know how to find the goal that I so greatly desired—an indigenous church among this people in Central Asia. But now I realized that, like divine torches in the night sky, there were people who could point the way. People who would reveal to me their secrets, if I asked the right questions and started really listening.

As is true with all pilgrimages, this journey was beginning to teach me much about myself, probably much more than I would ever teach others.

As I began to walk this new trail, something else happened. For the first time I found myself willing to admit that I was not some religious expert, only a simple pilgrim. No more, no less. I did not know everything, and I finally did not feel like I had to.

CHAPTER EIGHT

Labin's Long Shadow

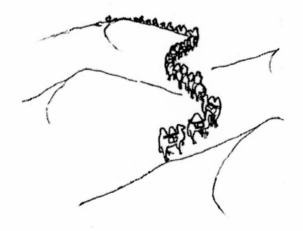

O ne of the things that pilgrims love to do along the trail is tell stories. The tales they spin are usually about people much like themselves. Stories full of devotion and faith, toil and danger, hardship and blessing.

Perhaps you are familiar with one of my favorites. It has many characters, the most memorable, and I might say, the most unpleasant of which is a Bedouin named Labin. If that name does not ring a bell, I am sure you will remember the protagonist of the story, a poor wandering pilgrim named Yacob. He is the center around which this pilgrim tale revolves, and no doubt you are familiar with his part in the story. But unknown to most, Yacob's manipulative father-in-law has lessons to teach us as well.

Leaving out two wives and two concubines, a herd of goats and a flock of children, the plot goes something like this. A powerful man named Labin sees the powerless young Yacob as a resource he can *use*. The older man skillfully manipulates events so that he can extract every last drop from the younger. Labin's personal ambition makes him blind to the divine purpose residing in his son-in-law. The story is a perfect illustration of the powerful *using* the weak, an image the pilgrim should never forget.

Several years ago I met another Yacob in Central Asia, but I refuse to say who *his* Labin was. This Yacob was also young, gifted, and bright. He had previously gone to a seminary far away to study theology, but now he was back and ready for ministry in his homeland.

This Central Asian Yacob had found himself a Raahel (thankfully, there is no Leah in this story) who was an outstanding evangelist in her own right. Considering the spiritual pedigree they carried as singles, everyone was expecting miracles from this young married couple.

Before the wedding bells had stopped ringing, various missionaries were in a lively competition for the use of their combined gifts. As a natural administrator, Yacob could prove a great help at any mission office, and Raahel's gift of evangelism would be a blessing anywhere.

The winning bidder was a pilgrim who had planted a small church but now was ready to move on. In a whirlwind decision, Yacob was installed as pastor and given a small salary to prove it. It appeared to be the crowning moment of a missionary church-planting effort—the baton being passed from a pilgrim who was leaving the field to a gifted local leader who would carry on the work.

Whenever a dynamic foreign missionary is in charge of a church, there will always be ready sources of foreign cash such as organizational money or the open wallets of short-term pilgrims. But once a local like Yacob takes over, money can become as scarce as shade on the Steppe. Furthermore, the pilgrim who was leaving had a charismatic personality that drew thirsty people like a spring of fresh water. Yacob, although outgoing and friendly, could never live up to the size of those footprints. Worst of all, it seems that no one had asked Yacob and Raahel what *their* vision for ministry might be. Did *they* really feel called to pastor this church?

The story becomes even more complicated. While busy trying to build up the little church, Yacob's administrative gift was still in demand. And since his heart was as big as his gift, he often found himself doing the bidding of others. One missionary might need him to process visas for his friends, another to help plan a project. Whenever a pilgrim needed the help of a skilled and diligent administrator, Yacob's phone rang. One day he would be looking after the flock he had been given, the next making arrangements for a short-term team. A few weeks later, he could be planning a conference for someone. There is nothing wrong with any of this, except that none of these things had sprung from Yacob's own heart.

Before long, our tale turns tragic, filled with defeat and heartbreak. Since the baton Yacob and Raahel had been passed was not their vision, the church soon folded. This seems to happen whenever someone attempts to fulfill another person's dreams—especially at the expense of their own.

It seems that we pilgrims usually don't ask local leaders what their visions are because we are too busy thinking about our own. We find it easier to *use* them as a means to reach our dreams than to help them explore theirs.

This is dangerous ground for the pilgrim, for once we start *using* hard-working local believers as a cheap labor to build our shrines and caravansaries, we have become no different from the worthless character Labin, whom we encountered at the beginning of this tale. Sometimes I fear that we have unwittingly become accustomed to using people in our religious structures back home, where accomplishments are more important than relationships. God's flock can easily become just another means to a self-glorifying end.

It should be obvious to the sincere pilgrim that using people is no way to build a *community*, but like many other things that should be obvious, this can be hidden by our personal agendas. Worse yet, when we act like modern-day Labins, we leave lingering shadows that will haunt the future of the indigenous church and its leadership.

You might be wondering what happened to Yacob and Raahel. After their church closed, the rumor mill churned with speculation. Some pilgrims searched for some secret sin that the couple must have been hiding. Others assumed they were just plain lazy. But worst of all was the ugly label whispered around town—that they were *failures.* A few of the pilgrims who had previously admired them went so far as to warn others to steer clear of Yacob, as if he had something contagious.

Perhaps Yacob and Raahel *had* failed, but at what? Fulfilling someone else's dreams? Instead, should we not ask: Who had failed *them*? Who had failed them by acting a little too much like Labin and *using* them rather than encouraging them to pursue their own calling?

Thankfully, in the dry air of Central Asia most wounds heal quickly. Yacob and Raahel were soon strong enough to do what few are willing to even consider. They moved to an untouched region and started over, deciding that it was better to pioneer than to plod along on someone else's path.

It is still too early to tell what the results will be, for this brave young couple has been called to toil in some very hard soil. But I have a feeling that their new ministry will bear fruit because they are finally walking in their own calling. Yet to do that, they had to walk so far from Labin's long shadow that no one could *use* them except God alone.

CHAPTER NINE

Funerals

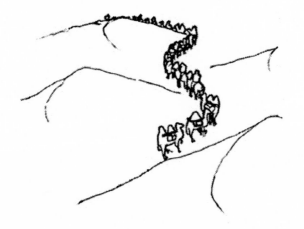

$\mathcal{T}$ he reason pilgrims need impressive blazing lights in the night sky is because it is so easy to get lost in Central Asia. Easy, that is, except when one might want to be lost. When you have a dozen phone calls to make and an ocean of emails demanding a reply, perhaps the best thing you can do is to get lost for a day or two.

We all need days when we can wander about like there is nothing important demanding our attention. Or at least, nothing as important as a good friend. In moments like this, Central Asia reveals her hidden treasures—treasures that may prove to be another fire tower.

On this particular agenda-less day in October, I managed to stumble across a dear friend. This took some serious wandering since he lives over two hundred miles away. Given the current condition of the Silk Road, this distance is so great that we only see each other when one of us manages to stray really far from our daily responsibilities.

Saeed shepherds a small group of believers in a city that is as close to the ends of the earth as most will ever see. His efforts in this city have earned him the respect of all who know him—friend and critic alike. In addition, he works full-time as a schoolteacher, while juggling the responsibilities of being a husband and father. Saeed certainly has more than enough to keep him busy, but true to his culture, he is never too busy for a wandering guest.

As always, he welcomed me into his home with a warm hug and immediately put on some water for tea. From the beginning of our visit, however, I sensed that Saeed was distracted. His voice was softer than usual and it sometimes trailed off before he had finished his thought. His eyes were often averted to the window, looking out into the distance rather than at me. This was not his usual self. It did not offend me, but I knew something was wrong.

Somewhere around the fifth cup of tea Saeed told me that his father had been in the hospital for the past few weeks. Just the day before, the doctors had informed the family that he was in the advanced stages of cancer.

Outside of a miracle, which they were praying for, there was little hope of recovery.

I now understood why my friend was so uncharacteristically quiet. An impending death in the family would make anyone this way, but for Saeed there was even more to it. Over the next week I watched events unfold that opened to me a new cultural insight, one that would be another heavenly sign along my journey.

Saeed was planning to bring his father home so they could care for his needs better. He also wanted the opportunity to read the Bible to him without a daily struggle with Muslim opposition at the hospital. His father was not a believer, but he seemed to be getting close to faith in Isa as Savior.

The next morning after breakfast, Saeed invited me for a walk. As we stepped outside, he slipped his hand into mine. My head understands that in Central Asia this is a sign of a strong brotherly bond, but I have yet to overcome my visceral reaction to holding hands with another man. Once again I chose to make the gigantic cross-cultural leap and walk hand-in-hand with Saeed through his neighborhood, all the while reminding myself that I am in *his* world, not mine.

Wandering through the mud streets, Saeed posed a deeply personal request which explained the intimate nature of our walk. In case his father did not pull through, would I be willing to call a few of the brothers? Saeed wanted me to contact the other believers from across the region because he knew his family would need all the support they could get, for death is one of those moments when Islam flexes its muscle.

When someone dies in Central Asia, the Islamic community takes over the funeral. Practically, that means the older members of the family and some leaders from the mosque handle the event. Traditional burial rites and certain ancient practices must be followed, and only the keepers of these traditions can be trusted to do them right. But this was not what my friend wanted for his father.

Saeed was, of course, hoping that it would not end this way. He was hoping that God, in His mercy, would somehow rescue his father from death. And rescue He did, but not as my friend had thought. When the cancer took its toll, it was a weary, but now *former* Muslim, who got promoted. At peace with his family, and also with God, Saeed's father passed on to life eternal.

But his father's death brought Saeed face-to-face with a serious dilemma. As pastor in his city for the past five years, he was a recognized follower of Isa and therefore, a well-known traitor to Islam. There was no way the mosque would help with this funeral. Or if they did, they would extract a high emotional price for their services.

In Central Asia, dying can be risky business for those who have turned to Isa as Savior. There are some thorny issues that arise. Issues such as *who* will bury you? And *where* will they bury you? For that matter, how can anyone do it properly besides the folks at the mosque, who are the ones that have always buried people? These are weighty questions in a culture that honors its ancestors.

On top of that, funerals are not a small affair in this part of the world. It takes quite a crew to pull one off properly. Several people are needed to wash and prepare the body for the last rites. The occasion calls for a team of men to dig the grave, as well as several women to do the cooking. Yet all this must be done by the end of the day following the death.

Up to this point, the few believers who had died were still controlled by their Muslim families. The families and the mosque had done everything, conducting the funerals in strict observance of Islamic traditions. The Muslim community had worked hard, and threatened much, in an attempt to hide the eternal realities of those believers' lives.

For years this issue had hung like an enormous sword over the very young church. Now someone was going to publicly face its edge.

Strangely, I never heard of any missionary losing sleep over the funeral question. In fact, I don't know if we missionaries had given much thought to it at all. I know I never had. Perhaps that is why pilgrims need someone else to build the torches that light the sky of our journey?

While none of us had given much thought to funerals, several of our local brothers and sisters had. Once I started calling around, I found that they were ready and knew exactly what to do. When word got out that Saeed's father had died, a living, breathing, caring body kicked into motion. More than forty believers, from four different cities, showed up ready to work.

Some men came with shovels and work clothes, and no one had to tell them how to dig a proper grave. A fellowship in another city sent money to cover the cost of feeding the two hundred guests expected, who would eat for three days. One group of women brought a mound of extra dishes because they knew that no one family would have enough. All of this was normally the duty of the mosque, but now it was being done by the body of Christ as it acted like a community. And believe me, the Muslims around them took notice.

To even the casual observer, it was obvious that these people knew what was, and what was not, a proper funeral. In many ways it looked like an ordinary Muslim funeral in their culture, but at certain important points, it was altogether different.

This was the first time a young national church had the chance to handle a funeral without interference from the crowd at the mosque, and the believers would use this moment to shine an eternal light. Saeed chanted a song of mourning over his father's dead body. But this time, the reading was found in the book of Job, and not the Koran. The men stretched out their hands over the grave and commended the soul to eternity, but this time it was done in the name of Him who sits at the right hand of the throne of God, and not Mohammed.

Before this extraordinary funeral was over, four of the Muslims present chose to leave Islam and follow this

Isa they were hearing about. Most probably this happened because they were hearing about Him in a way they hadn't before. No one was preaching in a meeting or giving out a booklet. The Muslim community was watching another community of faith care for its own. This produced a thunderous testimony in front of their culture.

Community and the Indigenous Church

Alongside this powerful witness, God was doing something else in their midst. Late into the night of the funeral more than a dozen men, all of them followers of Isa, sat together and discussed how they should now live. The Islamic community surrounding them is tightly-knit. When people come out of it, they need something new, yet similar, to be a part of. They don't need a church meeting to attend once or twice a week. They need a community.

So often we have asked people to give up their close-knit communities without offering them anywhere else to take refuge. For the individualistic Westerner this might be fine, but for someone coming out of Islam it is like asking them to stand in the street naked. We cannot keep ripping people out of their community and expecting that they will survive.

Some of my fellow pilgrims must be thinking, "Hey, what's all this talk about community? You said this was leading us toward the indigenous church." Don't worry, it still is—but of course that depends on what exactly we call a "church."

Most of the pilgrims I have known, myself included, subconsciously define "church" as a meeting. Meetings on Sundays. Meetings in mid-week. Probably an extra prayer meeting or two, if we are really spiritual.

But meetings do not bury people, communities do.

Meetings cannot host a proper wedding, but communities can.

In fact, there is a whole range of important things that meetings cannot do, things that only a community can. The idea of *community* is so important in Central Asian culture that they even have a special word for it, *Jamiat*, a word that does not translate well into English.

Perhaps that is why we often don't get it? Maybe that is why we need huge blazing lights in the night sky to point the way? At the very least, it is good reason why we should stop trusting in ourselves so much.

As the details of that funeral faded, my understanding sharpened. A meeting might be a fashionable place to stop. It might be a comfortable place for weary pilgrims to rest, but only a *community* living out life in full view of its surprised Muslim neighbors would be like a towering fire visible for hundreds of miles across the desert sky. It would point the way towards something of greater value than the shrines or caravansaries that we pilgrims tend to build. And it would point the way to the One who said at the funeral of a friend,

I am the Resurrection and the Life.

CHAPTER TEN

Hassan's Advice

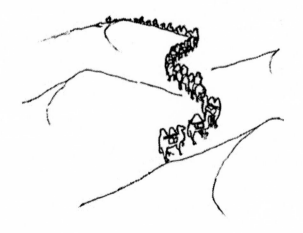

$\mathcal{P}$ilgrimages, we have already noted, are ancient affairs. Made for various reasons and to a myriad of places, they stretch across the pages of recorded history. If we are looking for them, they seem to appear out of nowhere. Take, for example, this fragment of a story preserved by a famous physician named Luke.

> *Every year his parents went to Jerusalem for the Feast of the Passover. When he was twelve years old, they went up to the Feast, according to their custom. After the Feast was over, while his parents were returning home, the boy Jesus stayed behind in Jerusalem…After three days they found him in the temple courts, sitting among the teachers, listening to them and asking them questions. Everyone who heard him was amazed at his understanding and his answers.*

Here we read of a simple and seemingly unlearned pilgrim, only about twelve years old, who amazed the learned religious professionals of his day. Does that surprise you?

From time to time, the wise and learned of this world are taught by the simple. Against all odds, the powerful are sometimes confounded by the weak. But when this happens things can get very ugly. But for those details, you will need to read the rest of Dr. Luke's story. Which, of course, is not a bad idea. The pilgrim will certainly find the ancient physician's story instructive, for history has a way of repeating itself. This is especially true if one ever considers trading in their unadorned pilgrim's cloak for the fine robes of a teacher.

The dilemma of what is proper apparel for the pilgrim has been a recurring question during my missionary pilgrimage in Central Asia. I don't try to be unorthodox, it just seems to happen on its own, especially when I start asking the question, "Who should be wearing the teacher's robe?"

Take the time I asked my friend Hassan to come speak at the year-end planning session of our missions' team. Inviting a local believer to teach missionaries is about as heretical as it gets, but I was not trying to be a rebel. I had sound reasons for wanting our team to connect with him. As one of the more mature Central Asian church leaders I knew, Hassan had a wealth of ministry experience. He had already been following Isa for a number of years. I was sure it would do our team good to see things through his eyes, if only a little. I just did not know what we would see.

That morning Hassan started with the story of how he came to know Isa as Savior. After that, however, he seemed unsettled and reluctant to continue. This seemed curious to me since Hassan is usually self-confident when he speaks. During a short tea break, Hassan reminded me that this was the first time he had met this group. Or, as he said, "I really don't know who they are."

I gently told him that what he had already shared was good, and that the team was enjoying this interaction. This seemed to encourage him and he continued, sharing a little about life in a typical Muslim village and about his ministry in that context. But soon the unease returned to his voice.

On the spur of the moment, I decided that more tea was in order. While my teammates were briefly distracted, I urged Hassan to tell us whatever was on his heart. "Don't hold back," I urged. "We really do want to hear what you're thinking." Or so I told him.

"I am not sure what kind of people these missionaries are." He was referring to my teammates, and he did so in the tone of a question.

Central Asians often do not speak their minds because their culture requires them to honor guests at all times. In the past, I had often seen the need to cultivate the idea that, as foreigners, we should consider it a privilege to be told the truth. It shows that we have become more than a guest to be honored; we are now a friend to be trusted.

I had also learned that Central Asians are experts at reading the eyes. If they pick up the message that someone is not interested in what they are saying, they will close down. If our eyes tell them that we don't respect their wisdom, they will not offer it. They seem to intrinsically follow the advice Jesus once gave His disciples,

Don't give your pearls to swine!
They will trample the pearls, then turn and attack you.

What Hassan did not know was that I was wrestling with the same fear as he was. Neither of us knew how my colleagues would react if he said something that didn't fit the paradigm of their seminary training. Some of them had studied for years and were well-versed in the principles of cross-cultural mission. Would they smile condescendingly at his naïve ideas? Would they reject, or even attack, this unpretentious village man because he did not understand the "real world" of missions?

My mind snapped back to the present, to my wistful friend Hassan, who was waiting for an answer. So with unspoken reservations, I told him that we were all simple souls, pilgrims at heart. We would listen.

Had I lied? Would we, the wise and learned, be willing to be taught by the simple? Would we, the powerful, be willing to listen to the weak? My fears were all the greater because I had no idea what Hassan wanted to say. Yet somehow, I knew that whatever it was, it would be significant.

At that moment none of us realized how close we were to an important revelation. If we kept our eyes and hearts open, we would soon see a sign. We would discern another of those great fire towers built for wandering pilgrims. In His tender mercy, God was about to allow another glimpse into the shape of an indigenous church in Central Asia. If only we would see it.

Despite my assurances, it took Hassan a few minutes to summon his courage. But once he did, his words became direct and honest. After what had been a careful Central Asian dance of words, he now felt free to tell us the truth. Thus transformed, he became a man on a mission.

"Our believing community is so small," he began. "How can we stand in the face of Islam if we are divided? We can barely survive when we are all together. But we can never stand up to Islam if we are divided into these churches."

Building toward a moment of truth, he added, "These 'churches' are your divisions. You brought them here and gave them to us. They are not ours. You started them, we didn't. They have been a means for you to divide and control us."

Everyone was listening politely, but the atmosphere became tense as Hassan continued. "There was never a need to build separate little churches. Satan has used all this to bring division between the brothers here. These different names on your churches have only brought your divisions to us."

The pain in his voice was tangible, and years of bottled-up tears formed syllables as he spoke. Hassan was revealing the true heart of a shepherd. He longed to see the body of Christ grow strong in Central Asia. He yearned to see his people thrive spiritually in this difficult place, but a thoroughly Western idea of church was standing in the way.

Bible idea

Imported Pain

In spite of numerous Scripture passages to the contrary, we missionaries had modeled that division of the body was acceptable. We had built structures that compelled each little group of believers to have its own nicely ordered weekly meeting. After all, is that not the proper definition of church?

Yet to mature believers like Hassan, a church is much more than a meeting. It is a *community*. Singular. Here was someone saying the unthinkable. He was proposing that "church in the plural" does not translate well for Central Asia. Hassan was saying that you cannot have many churches for the same reason that one person can't have many bodies. He even seemed to imply that the age-old missionary practice of carving up territories, and then bragging about our numbers, was all wrong. Maybe even sin?

I might be unorthodox in some ways, but this was hard even for me to take. If forty-seven separate churches in my small hometown is good enough for Christians in the American Bible belt, why would it not work for believers in Central Asia?

Without thinking, we had simply given them what we brought from home. Our love for head counts. Our quarrels. Our divisions. I doubt that most of us had ever even asked if there might be another, more fitting way for worship and witness in this culture.

By our example we had inadvertently taught that Western forms and expressions of Christianity are the only right ones, even when they are clearly going against Scripture. Moreover, in just a few short years, these ideas had spawned spiritual pride. The ugly kind of spiritual pride that I once overheard bragging, "Our pastor is more anointed than your pastor."

This nasty legacy left the local body of Christ fractured and fighting for its life. It was the cause of the pain in Hassan's voice. Over the years he had grown weary of watching a divided body fall, again and again.

Hassan was also tired of seeing the ones he loved search for their strength and structure in the wrong places. To anyone willing to listen, he was graciously saying that the time had come to stop mindlessly following the ideas of foreign missionaries. It was time to begin looking for answers in the normal patterns of life in Central Asia. Could this be the meaning of *indigenous?*

This probably would not have bothered us had we still been only unpretentious pilgrims. Ah, but somewhere along the journey things had changed. We had now become the wise and learned ones. In the eyes of most local believers, we missionaries are the religious professionals. No one ever quite said it, but somehow everyone knows that when it comes to church, we have all the answers. A pilgrim can easily start liking it this way, making change that much harder.

Unfortunately for us, a few people like my friend Hassan were starting to see our blind spots. Our fine robes of religious pride no longer fooled them. A few Central Asian leaders were beginning to recognize what we pilgrims could not—the need for community. Most of us missionaries had come from individualistic cultures, and therefore, we could not even perceive the problem, much less cure it.

Not only did Hassan instinctively recognize the problem we had created, he also knew the cure.

> *How good and pleasant it is*
> *when brothers live together in unity!*
> *It is like the precious oil poured on the head,*
> *running down on the beard,*
> *running down on Aaron's beard,*
> *down upon the collar of his robes...*
> *For there the LORD bestows his blessings,*
> *even life forevermore.*

A broken, divided body was in need of some healing balm from this pilgrimage song composed by King David. The local body of Christ, this community as Hassan called it, needed the Lord to bestow His blessings on them. In fact, these brothers and sisters needed the blessings that would come from unity more than they needed to please their beloved missionary friends. Why couldn't we "religious professionals" seem to understand this?

I guess that is why God turns the tables from time to time. He allows the simple to teach the wise and learned. He allows the weak to confound the powerful. Moreover, when He does, it is a sign. As sure as a great blazing light in the nighttime sky, it can breathe new life into the lost pilgrim. It can produce hope for all who are willing to see it, for it tells us that the great Sovereign who rules our journey has not abandoned us to stumble in the dark on our own.

Best of all, once you begin to see these signs, they are all around.

CHAPTER ELEVEN

Tea Party Terrorists

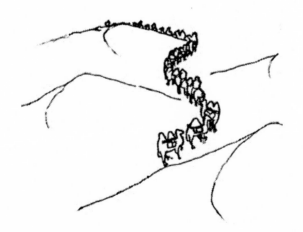

*O*ne of the occupational hazards for a pilgrim in Central Asia is terrorism. It is not a new phenomenon in this part of the world. From ancient times, bandits and other lawless characters have roamed the same roads as pilgrims, spreading fear and anxiety. It does not happen often, but just one run-in with these dreadful fanatics can ruin your life. If you are not careful, they might even maim your theology.

Sitting together for three or four hours at a time drinking tea, eating, and laughing at awful jokes—this is what decent Central Asian men commonly do for fun. So it was that a group of friends began to meet every month or so in this time-honored pattern. One can easily imagine a band of Muslim terrorists gathering in the same way, covertly planning their next hit over a cup of tea. But these seven or eight men were not religious terrorists—even if it might seem that way to you later.

Each man regularly attends one of the big-city style Western churches that had been planted in our city. This experience alone qualified the men for the following assault better than any training they could have received in Afghanistan.

One evening, somewhere between a second plate of rice and the third cup of tea, the conversation turned to matters more serious. Someone very casually laid it on the table. A nasty religious bomb, that is. The ticking of its timer sounded something like this:

"We all know we can't bring our unbelieving friends and family into our churches. They are far too Western. One visit would prove to them that we have left our people and become Christians."

Please forgive my friends for their dislike of the word "Christian." For them, it does not evoke the warm and fuzzy feelings that it does for many in the West. In Central Asia, "Christian" translates something like "worshipers of a strange Russian god." Beyond that, their definition includes some other ideas that I am embarrassed to mention.

As former Muslims, the men seated at the table intrinsically knew this. In fact, they seemed to know a great deal about following Isa in Central Asia. Perhaps that is why each one quickly added his own comments about what a strange and inhospitable place a church meeting could be.

If there had been several missionaries in the room, this is exactly when the bomb would have detonated. *Kaboom*! Theology degrees and Bible school diplomas would have been blown to smithereens.

Then someone dared to go further. "Since these meetings don't seem to reach our own people, what else can we do?" he asked.

In military terminology this would be called a secondary blast. It was probably a premeditated effort to clear the room of any residual Western theology.

However, it must be remembered that this was not a room full of missionaries with agendas and methodologies to defend. These men were simply former Muslims who now loved Isa—men who only wanted more of their kinsmen to do the same. It did not matter one whit to them what we may have been taught in preparation for this pilgrimage. The theories used in seminaries and Bible colleges are unknown to them. In fact, I doubt any of them had ever contemplated the question, "What is an indigenous church?" I know they had not read the latest books on the subject.

Yet just stop to consider how well qualified they were to discuss this matter. First, they were themselves former Muslims. They personally understood what goes on in the mind of a Central Asian man the first time he encounters organized Christianity. Second, they knew full well what it was like to inwardly accuse yourself of being a traitor every time you entered a church.

Perhaps even more significantly, they did not feel the need to defend the status quo. They politely assaulted it. The church traditions imported by their Western friends were like the pilgrims who brought them—strangers and aliens to this land. This was something these men could see clearly.

True to their Eastern heritage, they had been exceptionally respectful to their guests. Proper hospitality is immensely important in their worldview. Nevertheless, deep inside they all knew the time had come. Even in Central Asia, sooner or later it is time for friends and their traditions to go home.

What these men may have lacked in theological training they made up for in wisdom—the kind of wisdom that comes from simply living your whole life in Central Asia. They may not have known the Bible as well as their educated pilgrim friends, but they could see something most of us did not. These followers of Isa knew that something needed to change about the way "church" was being done. But they also realized that few missionaries would be willing to hear their extremist views.

I know these guys. They are all noble and peace-loving. They would never intentionally hurt the pilgrims they know and love. However, even a hint of such radical ideas would be considered religious terrorism by many missionaries.

Only time will tell if these men will be dismissed as dangerous heretics, or hailed as heroes of the faith. But then again, there are many things that are only revealed with the passage of time. And some things will remain hidden until eternity.

CHAPTER TWELVE

Wind, Sand, and Time

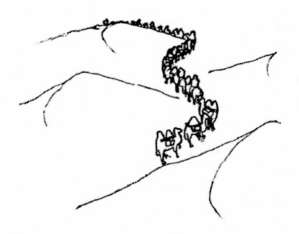

C entral Asia can be a dangerous place to build. Structures often don't last. For centuries past, and even now, the prime building material has been mud-brick. No matter how grand a structure's design or how exquisitely ornamented it may be, the deadly combination of wind, sand, and time will prove devastating to such materials.

I guess that's the way it is with most things men build.

> Unless the Lord builds a house,
> its builders labor in vain.

This is a shame, for great labor goes into building. Sometimes a large measure of vanity is included as well. That may not always be the case, but self-importance can be quite an architect. Of course, only God knows who built what, and only He will judge each one's work for what it is.

Yet there is a good side to this mud-brick construction. For when these structures wear away, they always leave something behind—dirt. And usually, the only thing required for this transformation is the passage of time.

A man's hard work, his plans, and his sacrifice frequently return to their most basic element, awaiting someone else's vision to shape them. It is good that Central Asia is thus constituted, for it is full of the fallen structures that were once so important to a previous builder. Upon their ruin, these elements provide the raw materials for those who come later.

I have a Central Asian friend who is well acquainted with wind-worn and ruined structures. In less than a decade of faith in Christ, Bakir and his wife Gulya have been leaders in two churches that the winds blew into the dustbin of history. Both churches had been driven by the visions of courageous people. Courageous foreign pilgrims, to be exact. But each of them disintegrated because of those two words—*foreign* and *pilgrim*.

The first church wore away mostly because it was foreign—foreign funded, with a foreign style of worship.

It was foreign in its essential nature, with nothing indigenous about it. Nor had there been any real attempt to make it so. Such was that pilgrim's vision. But all things foreign, even those things grand and wonderful, are especially vulnerable to the effects of wind and time. The lifestyle promoted by easy foreign money can wear away a local pastor's heart and harden his character, problems that a monthly salary and an impressive building cannot overcome.

The second church died—a most accurate description—precisely because it was the vision of a pilgrim. A kind and deeply committed pilgrim to be sure, but a pilgrim nonetheless. As is the case with all pilgrims, the day came when he had to leave. And when he did, the little church he had built around his loving personality succumbed to the cruelty of the elements.

It may be a short time, or it may be decades. It may even be in a coffin, but there always comes a day when the pilgrim goes home. And when this deeply committed pilgrim left, the church he had labored so hard to build simply died a natural death.

Bakir and Gulya had given a piece of their hearts to these churches and therefore grieved over their demise. But still worse was the way their foreign leaders acted on the day when their work was tested. Even the best of pilgrims can turn harsh and accusing upon seeing their plans, hard work, and sacrifice returning to the dust from which it was drawn.

> *Unless the Lord builds a house,*
> *its builders labor in vain.*

Could it be that the vanity of building great structures is only exceeded by the arrogance displayed when they fall to ruin?

Bruised and sore, Bakir and Gulya came close to packing up their dreams and heading back to the worldly ways of Central Asia. Only by the grace of God did they stand firm. A small flame still burned in their hearts, and that gave them the courage to build on their own. When they did, they discovered that their dreams and desires were a heavenly blueprint for something different.

They realized that foreigners often need great buildings to sustain their visions. Bakir and Gulya decided to be content with humble houses to enclose theirs. Their foreign friends had drawn grand and elaborate designs, but simple sketches would be enough for them.

With a clear sense of calling, they began to survey what was left. In both places where they had once worshiped, spiritual desert had again taken over. Where splendid foreign-looking structures had stood, they now found mounds of broken and eroded brick. Lives that had taken the brunt of the collapse of foreign constructions lay scattered in the debris.

It did not seem that much was left lying around in these ruins, but with what little there was, Bakir and Gulya started re-building. The foreigners had built structures with logic they could understand but local believers could not. For Bakir it came naturally to build with simple stories and prophet-like challenges that make most foreigners uncomfortable. Without stopping to think about it, the two of them set their hands to build by a different design.

As they did, Bakir struggled with feeling incompetent as a builder, which was due partly to the fact that his mistakes were many. However, this was also caused by issues beyond his control. How could he have known that while we pilgrims enjoy receiving respect, we are sometimes unwilling to return the favor? Who would have guessed that the very act of picking up the pieces would be perceived as a threat to the status quo?

At that particular moment in his life, it was essential for Bakir to sense that he had the respect of others if he was going to overcome his own fear and inexperience. He especially needed it from the many missionaries whom he admired. Unfortunately, it does not always work this way in the competitive business of building private kingdoms.

In spite of it all, Bakir and Gulya are slowly succeeding where others ultimately failed. They will never achieve renown as the builders of great buildings, but where the passage of time had brought back the desert of spiritual darkness, there are again small springs of hope. Where foreigners had built their grand structures, they have built and are continuing to build spiritual household after household—small *communities* of faith in a corner of Central Asia.

Perhaps the fierce combination of wind and time may someday erode their work as well. That is certainly possible. But I get the feeling that what Bakir and Gulya are building will survive much better than the grand designs of pilgrims. For theirs are humble structures and unpretentious plans, which seem better suited to the ravages of Central Asia. For that reason they may do more than simply survive. Perhaps they will even prosper.

Again, only time will tell.

CHAPTER THIRTEEN

Poplar Trees

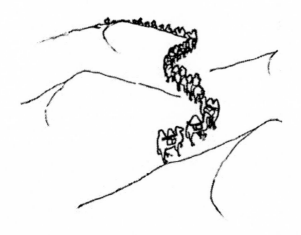

He is like a tree planted by streams of water,
which yields its fruit in season,
and whose leaf does not wither.
Whatever he does prospers.

*T*hese words call to mind a classic sight in Central Asia—a row of stately poplar trees lining some dusty back road. Those who have traveled the region will instantly recognize the image, for nothing is as typical of the Central Asian countryside.

In almost every city, and in all the little towns and villages, countless streets are framed with long, straight rows of poplars. Always elegantly planted in straight lines, their distinctive shape symbolizes the normal order of life in Central Asia. The symmetrical rows call to mind the tradition-ordered culture that planted them, and the trees' proximity to each other projects the intimate sense of community that pervades life here.

No matter where in Central Asia our pilgrimage might take us, the poplar will be there. They grow in the farthest northern reaches where the winters plunge to forty degrees below zero. They thrive along the smallest spring of water on the southern rim of the Taklamakan Desert where it only rains once a year. You can plant them in vast numbers and actually expect that most of them will survive. They require little care because they are native to Central Asia. Their leaf does not wither because they are indigenous. They prosper because they belong.

Unlike the pilgrim, who is only traveling through, a poplar tree is rooted to its own environment. The sand, winds, and weather have shaped these trees to be what they are. These icons of Central Asia reflect generations of interaction with the elements around them.

As a pilgrim who has traveled many a mile on Central Asian back roads, I have come to love these long, straight rows. One of my most cherished memories is that of driving through two lines of poplars in the golden glowing of a fading desert sunset. All these years later the image still fills me with delight.

Something about the poplars silently speaks to me. Deep down inside I take comfort in them as one does in the face of an old friend. Their distinctive order helps me find my bearings, for they personify Central Asia for me. They are, more than anything else I know, truly indigenous here.

Trees and symmetry are obviously not the reason I started on this pilgrimage, and they do not keep me here. But traveling along a road lined by poplars makes me feel like I might be going somewhere, that my life is headed in the right direction.

The idea of "going somewhere" is a high value in the cultures from which most pilgrims come. But for my friends Akim Jan and Rena, nothing could have been further from their minds when they first believed in their Savior Isa. Like everyone around them, this couple was simply trying to survive the collapse of the latest empire to rule Central Asia.

They had been Muslims—not very good ones, but Muslims nonetheless. Their lives had been predictable and orderly, but suddenly their world turned upside down. While their country was in the throes of economic ruin, my friends found a clean, pure spring on the side of life's road. It was to them

a spring of water welling up to eternal life.

Akim Jan and Rena had met Isa, the One who had said,

Whoever believes in me, as the Scripture has said,
streams of living water will flow from within him.

But all this was strange and unfamiliar. In their own words, they knew basically nothing. Nothing, that is, except how to love people. Nothing, except how to speak about their Savior whenever there was an opportunity. Nothing, except how to pray for the sick, and perhaps cast out a demon when needed.

For the first year or so of their new life, Akim Jan and Rena simply did what came naturally to them. They read their Bible and did what it said. Slowly the spring they had found was starting to well up life all around them. It was as natural as growing poplars trees.

However, they didn't get some of the results that others thought they should and they were soon told that the life bubbling out of their home was not a church. No one could tell them exactly what it was, but it was definitely not a proper church.

So over the next few years, Akim Jan tried to do things properly. At times he was told to hold a "cell meeting" in his home. Other times he and Rena tried "planting a church." Neither proved easy with a new, fundamentalist Muslim seminary a few blocks away. Even so, they searched hard for the right road to ministry success.

Through this pursuit they learned that they needed to add some important new activities to what had previously been so natural:

1. Arrange for proper meetings, make them orderly, and finish on time.

2. Plan for proper worship times to begin these meetings; organize good singing with talented musicians.

3. Prepare proper sermons for these meetings, ones that have three points, interesting illustrations, and a clear application.

Akim Jan tried many of the goods being peddled by various well-intentioned pilgrims who traveled through his region. Big Church. Cell Church. He probably even tried a few other kinds of church, but none of them really fit.

The more they followed the models imported from the West, the more problems they faced. The mosque tried to rally a mob, and the KGB wanted to put Akim Jan in jail. Some of the new believers got accustomed to Western ways and started looking for a mission to employ them. The road just didn't open up like everyone had promised it would. It still hasn't.

Don't misunderstand. Akim Jan and Rena still witness healings and other miraculous signs. They continue to see numbers of Muslims come to believe and follow Isa, and their spiritual influence in the city grows every year. They are still faithfully shepherding these new believers through life's many difficulties and hardships. But they have never started a *church*. At least not one that looks anything like what many others thought it should.

Now, after five or six years of trying to make missionaries happy, they understand that to be a good thing. Akim Jan said it to me this way: "I don't want to build a big church. I don't want to build a bunch of small churches. I don't want to build a church at all. I want to grow a *community* of people who worship Isa."

Selah.

He explained to me that there are more important things in our faith than meetings and numbers. Things like a new *community* actually living out the words of their Master—loving their neighbors, forgiving their enemies, and bearing witness before the local authorities.

Somewhere along the way Akim Jan has found an answer, an authentically Central Asian answer. Or maybe he has simply recovered something they had lost. Akim Jan and Rena realized that what they were searching for would not be found in the fine-sounding theories of foreign pastors or their systems of church. What they desired could only be found closer to home. *Much* closer. After years of trying to plant many other things, I think he decided to stick with poplars.

Akim Jan came to understand that if a church is to be truly indigenous, it will reflect years of interaction with the elements around it. If it is going to survive the extremes of spiritual weather, it must be rooted in its own unique environment.

Sounds like a tall order, but what if it were to happen? What if Akim Jan, and others like him, merely raised up *communities* of people who worship Isa? And what if these *communities* symbolized everything good about the normal order of life in Central Asia?

They would then grow in the farthest of the northern reaches where the winters plunge to forty degrees below zero. Yet they would still thrive along the smallest spring of water on the southern rim of the Taklamakan Desert, where it only rains once a year. We would see vast numbers of such *communities* started, and actually expect that most of them would survive. They would require little care because they would be native. They would yield their fruit in season, and their leaf would not wither, because they would be indigenous. Such a *community* of people who follow Isa will prosper in Central Asia because it will grow like a poplar tree in its native soil.

As one who has traveled many a mile on Central Asian back roads, this will undoubtedly be the most cherished memory of my missionary pilgrimage.

CHAPTER FOURTEEN

A Time for Everything

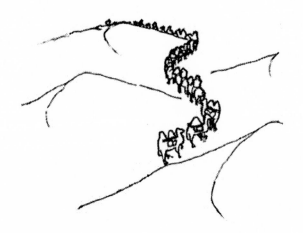

$\mathcal{K}$ing Solomon, who purportedly made a pilgrimage to Central Asia, once wrote:

There is a time for everything,
and a season for every activity under the heaven.

Our royal fellow pilgrim was right. Everything, no matter how good or how bad, will someday come to an end. I guess, by his use of the word "everything," we have to assume that it includes pilgrimages?

Even in difficult places like Central Asia, we eventually arrive at the goal of our journey when we see this awe-inspiring thing called an indigenous church. The mere thought of that day has given us joy as we traveled through arid lands. Its image, flickering just beyond the horizon, drove us on when a weary spirit was urging us to quit.

Yet, when this moment of rejoicing comes into view, we are also faced with some disturbing questions: Just what should a pilgrim *do* at the end of a pilgrimage? Is it right for the pilgrim to stay on a while? And if they *do* stay, exactly how should pilgrims act in this new role?

At this difficult moment of transition, it is important that we remember the signs we have already seen. And God has graciously shown us many. Each of these, as diverse as they have been, share one thing in common: They were all found while spending time with Central Asian friends.

The fire towers that lighted our way in the desert did not come from lectures in a classroom. These insights were not the product of our intellect. They came into view only when we took the time to listen—to listen to the wisdom that comes from simply living your whole life in Central Asia. Therefore, it is only fitting that we should find our bearings in this moment of transition while doing what we have often done before—drinking tea with a friend.

I went to see Talgat mainly because that is what friends do in Central Asia—spend time together. He is not a ministry project, but a friend whose company I enjoy. Nevertheless, I also wanted to see him because I knew Talgat was struggling with problems in his ministry, and I thought that he might need someone to talk to. Little did I know that what he needed to say was exactly what I needed to hear.

My friend Talgat is a typical Central Asian man— extremely loyal to his family, generally likeable, and not given to a lot of words. In other ways though, he is most extraordinary. For a start, he has been a follower of Isa for more than seven years. Few of his people fit that description. Not only that, but he has exercised authentic Christian leadership for most of that time. He doesn't carry a title like "Pastor" or "Reverend," but he is the sort of man Paul wrote about in his first letter to the young Timothy:

> *The overseer must be above reproach, the husband of but one wife, temperate, self-controlled, respectable, hospitable, able to teach, not given to drunkenness, not violent but gentle, not quarrelsome, not a lover of money. He must manage his own family well and see that his children obey him with proper respect.*

In Talgat's world, these qualities speak far louder than the seminary degree others aspire to. Maybe that is the way it should be.

As with every other significant conversation I've had in Central Asia, this one began and ended over a cup of tea, with a meal somewhere in between. Nothing is done or said in a hurry. All those who would take a pilgrimage into this land of Bactrian camels and Oriental carpets should remember that the nasty American habit of quickly getting down to business feels very rude in this part of the world.

Talgat and I sat in the living room where we ate and talked alone. For the most part, his wife Dilbahar kept to the kitchen. It was not for lack of something relevant to say, for at key moments she would briefly join us and share what was on her mind. But mixed company at a meal does not sit well with my friend, so one stern look was usually enough to return her to the kitchen.

Please don't judge him too harshly in this. Remember, we are the foreigners in his house. This is also a good reminder that Central Asia is an altogether different place from the West.

After the meal I tried to draw Talgat out, but to do so I would have to carefully watch my natural tendency toward directness. If I wanted to know what was going on inside this man, I would have to be discreet and indirect—an art I have yet to master.

I decided to begin by asking his thoughts on a couple of general ministry questions. I was certainly interested in the ideas of one who could rightly be called "a pillar of the church" in Central Asia. But more than that, I hoped my questions might start him talking about the more troubling things on his mind.

Talgat gave me a vague answer to the effect that they had "made good progress" over the past five or six years. There was still "much to do," but the groundwork had been done. Then, from out of nowhere, he asked me an odd, leading question: "How do you understand your work here? How do you define your role as a missionary?"

Remember, this question was coming from a man who had been a follower of Isa longer than I had lived in Central Asia. He had probably known as many missionaries as I have. Something important was lurking under the surface of his query.

Talgat must have noticed a puzzled look on my face, so he tried to clarify by saying that he had "never really understood Westerners," and wanted a clearer picture of how we think.

Since I had been trying to develop the art of being indirect, I decided not to give him a straight answer. I simply asked him to read some words from one of my favorite missionary thinkers:

> By the grace God has given me, I laid a foundation as an expert builder, and someone else is building on it. Each one should be careful how he builds.

After reading this passage, Talgat spent a few minutes in thought. Then he replied, "I think I'm getting a revelation of something here."

Looking back on the moment, I believe he had already given a great deal of thought to what he was about to say. He had meditated, if not specifically on this verse, certainly on the subject in general. Nevertheless, what followed was certainly a revelation for one person in the room.

"Paul was an apostle," said Talgat slowly, "which means he was a 'sent one.' He went around starting churches. So what he describes here is the way apostles, or 'sent ones,' are supposed to start churches. I've never seen this before, but it makes sense because Paul was explaining something that is normal in our culture."

I had to think quick. I had looked at the back pages of a Bible a lot during my Sunday School days, but I never saw a *Journeys of Saint Paul* map that included Central Asia. So how is it that Paul intersected with Central Asian culture? Talgat certainly had my attention.

"In traditional culture," he continued, "when someone wants to build a house, they invite all their friends and family to come help. On the appointed day, everyone comes ready to work—and work hard. They all know that with enough men, and one hard day's work, the foundation of a new house can be laid. So that is the focus. They do not worry about doing other things, the foundation is what they came to build. While the men are working, the women prepare a huge, traditional meal. But even though there is much to be done, it is much more than work. It's a celebration. A new house is going up."

As Talgat talked, I could picture the preparations I've watched many times for other big events like weddings or funerals. The men would be occupied with whatever needed to be done outside, while the women washed and cooked the rice, cut piles of carrots, and prepared the meat. It is the same at all big parties.

He continued painting his picture for me. "By late afternoon, the foundation is finished. Some of the men start cleaning up, while others quickly assemble a sort of long table for the feast. Soon there will be lots of eating, laughing, and drinking tea." As he was speaking I could see the men in my mind's eye, sweaty and bone-tired, but glowing with a sense of accomplishment from the day's labors.

"Later that night, when the eating, music, and dancing are over," continued Talgat, "the owner of the house stands up to profusely thank all who answered his call for help. He freely admits that he could never have done it without them, and ends by telling them that he is forever in their debt. They were there the day the foundation was laid."

Then in an unexpected anticlimax, Talgat finished his story. "And then everyone goes home."

I sat there startled; it seemed too abrupt. There had to be more to it, but when I pressed him on this point, Talgat's rationale went something like this: "The people came to do one thing—to lay the foundation. They did what could not have been done without their help. When that is finished, it is the owner's business to finish his own house." As much as I wanted something more, I could see the logic.

But this was not all. My friend was on a roll and he continued to expound his thoughts. "And just like Paul, you foreign missionaries are the helpers in our tradition. God called you from all over the world to come to Central Asia and help us lay the foundation. We never could have done it without you. But now that part is soon to be finished. It is almost time for us to prepare a great feast and tell you how much we appreciate all your hard work and sacrifice for our people."

My thoughts drifted back to the Apostle Paul's words, trying hard to apply them to Talgat's story and to the missionary practice I have seen in Central Asia. Then it dawned on me why Paul the church-planter did not stick around to finish the house. Why? *Because it is the owner's job to do so.*

Who better to decide where to put windows, or how many bedrooms are needed? Is it not the one who will live in it? Paul tells us that there is only one foundation that can be laid—Christ Jesus. But could many floor plans be built on this one foundation?

My mind was pulled back to the present by Talgat's voice. "And then you will all leave."

His directness caught me off-guard and I was silent for a moment.

"Is that how it works?" he pressed. "Will all the missionaries leave soon so we can build the church to look like we want?"

What could I say? How could I tell him that there is a right and proper way for some pilgrims to stay on past the foundation stage? Would he even consider that our partnership could be helpful long into the future? How might I explain the ideal scenario in which we foreigners move to the background while the "owners of the house" take the lead?

Indeed, how could I enlighten my friend to such idealistic church-planting theory when his experience had painted a much different picture? Missionaries fading into the background is a model he has seldom seen. Most missionaries can talk at length about such ideas as theory. Yet few church-planters are ready, in practice, to act like the Apostle Paul, truly risking the leadership of a new church into the hands of local believers.

However, I didn't need to tell my friend all this. He already knew. He had known for years. In fact, as I pondered on this issue, I realized that watching foreigners lord it over the local church has probably been the bitter root feeding most of Talgat's thorny ministry problems over the years. Could it be that this story was his polite, Central Asian way of telling me so?

For some strange reason, we foreign missionaries seem to forget that *we* are the pilgrims, the temporary ones. This land through which we sojourn, no matter how much we come to love it, is not our home. Our new brothers and sisters are the ones destined to live in the house. They, and their children after them, will have to deal with what we do, both good and bad. And because of our convenient memory lapses, we somehow believe that it is our right to perpetually stay on and supervise.

We would probably still be welcomed as helpers, but not as overlords. And that is precisely where the problem arises. Many missionaries have the hardest time moving out of the limelight and off to stage left. It's as if we don't really believe that God will work through our local brothers and sisters with the same power that He works though us. Could it be that sometimes our faith is in ourselves rather than in the Spirit of God?

Talgat was right. When the foundation is laid, this house, the indigenous church in Central Asia, should be finished by the ones who will live in it. Whatever continuing roles we foreigners may rightly fill, it is fundamentally different from that of local leadership.

They must be the ones, led by the Holy Spirit, who frame the windows and decide what color to paint the walls. In fact, that is the only way the church will ever truly be indigenous.

I left Talgat's house contemplating some uncomfortable questions. His words were a reminder that this pilgrimage, for me at least, was not about the many noble and progressive things we missionaries often do. Rather, it had been a search for only one thing, that marvelous Holy Grail we call an indigenous church.

Could it be that my quest was over?

EPILOGUE

The Treasures in My Bag

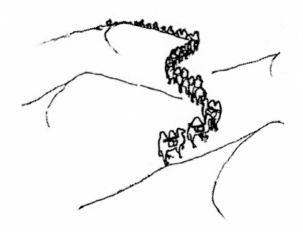

E very pilgrim carries a bag. Yes, I know the words of Him who sent out our early pilgrim brothers:

> *Go! I am sending you out like lambs among wolves.*
> *Do not take a purse or bag or sandals.*

I guess it is another admission of my failure when I say that I have not lived up to this command. I have carried a bag. And at times a purse full of money. As well as a few other things that Jesus did not warn His disciples about.

Maybe that is why the journey has been so hard at times. Was I carrying too much of a load? That will have to be left to conjecture, for you see, it looks like my little bag has now become empty.

I started out with so many things: my American prejudices, a thoroughly Western theology, some deeply personal fears, and a few delusions of grandeur. You name it. At the beginning of this journey my bag was so full that most would have called it *baggage*.

But I can only speak for myself; each pilgrim must decide for themselves what they will, or will not, carry. My advice is to be careful, for the seemingly little bag that most of us start out with may become painfully heavy in the future.

Despite a self-confident beginning, the steep mountain roads and blistering desert sands that I faced on my pilgrimage eventually had their way. Over time they caused the weight of my bag to become unbearable, forcing me to spill its contents, gradually emptying it at various places along the trail.

As all those once precious things spilled out, I found room for new, far more valuable ones. Without even thinking about it, I picked up a few items along the way. Every time I lost some cherished idea or trinket from home, I gained something priceless. And no, I am not talking about those exquisite Oriental carpets on my floor.

I am referring to the bits of what I hope has been wisdom, which I have tried to communicate in the pages of this book. For it happened that whenever I was willing to lay one thing down, I was given something to pick up in return. Something to provoke my thoughts in the late night hours when I could not sleep. Something that would make an eternal change in my ideas about life and ministry.

My bag slowly became re-filled with personal maps, markers, and a few stories that one pilgrim might pass on to another. Somehow these bits and pieces grew over time and eventually overflowed onto these pages.

Now it seems that I have come to the end of my notes, observations, and criticisms. I guess that means I am done. I am sure I could have learned more from those who were willing to teach me. And this is something for the wise pilgrim to always remember—there are people who are willing to teach us, if we are humble enough to listen.

However, since listening is a skill I picked up late, I doubt it took long for you to read the words of wisdom that have flowed from my pen. It can be somewhat disappointing when a man realizes that everything he has to say will fit on such few pages, but even so, I hope you enjoyed the journey.

As we prepare to part company, I am aware there might be several reasons that someone could be dissatisfied with this offering of mine. For example, it is possible that some of my fellow pilgrims were disturbed by my stories. I certainly hope so. They disturb me, but only when I slow down long enough to think—a good habit for the pilgrim to cultivate.

Some might think I was too hard on the missionaries in my stories. Maybe so, but more probably I was not hard enough. Remember, I am one of them. Therefore, I likely judged us less strictly than the One who will do so on the day our motives are exposed for all to see.

Or it could be this little work did not live up to the expectations raised by its title. It most certainly did not answer all the questions I provoked. Perhaps it didn't answer any of them.

In fact, I can almost hear some pilgrims protest, "You never answered the real question. You never explained what an indigenous church is supposed to look like."

But to be honest, I do not remember promising to do so. And by now it should be clear that I am really the wrong person to ask. Nevertheless, if in an arrogant moment I implied something like that in those first few chapters, I ask you to forgive me. I could not fulfill that vow if I tried. I can only plead for grace.

On the other hand, if that is the only real question—
"What should the indigenous church look like?"—I did
not need to write a book on the subject. It has already
been described quite well. In the first century, an old
man had a vision or something while exiled on an island
off the coast of Turkey:

> *I saw the Holy City, the new Jerusalem, coming
> down out of heaven from God, prepared as a bride
> beautifully dressed for her husband. And I heard a
> loud voice from the throne saying, "Now the
> dwelling of God is with men, and he will live with
> them. They will be his people, and God himself will
> be with them and be their God."*

If that's not the answer you were looking for, if you
wanted something realistic and concrete, may I make a
suggestion? First, put your books, degrees, and fine
teaching robes in storage—you may need them someday,
but not on this journey. Then, adorn yourself with the
humble cloak of a pilgrim; it holds your best hope of
someday arriving at the destination you so desire. And if
you must carry a bag, keep it light. It makes gathering
real treasures all the easier. Thus equipped, you can soon

join another outbound caravan. May God grant that your pilgrimage produces clearer answers than did mine.

But before we say goodbye, I would like to share with you, my fellow pilgrim, the one last treasure still lying in my bag. It does not belong to me any more than it does to anyone else, so I guess I am just passing it along. I leave you with the Master's words:

Peace be with you.
As the Father sent me, I am sending you.

SCRIPTURE CITED

All Scripture quotations are taken from the *Holy Bible, New International Version,* unless noted otherwise.

Prologue: *A Heart Set on Pilgrimage*
>Psalm 84:1–2, 5, & 10
>
>Isaiah 11:9 (KJV)

Chapter Two: *Point of Entry*
>Proverbs 16:18
>
>Proverbs 4:7

Chapter Five: *On Being Lost*
>Deuteronomy 8:2

Chapter Nine: *Funerals*
>John 11:25

Chapter Ten: *Hassan's Advice*
>Luke 2:41–43 & 46–47
>
>Matthew 7:6 (KJV)
>
>Psalm 133

Chapter Twelve: *Wind, Sand, and Time*
>Psalm 127:1

Chapter Thirteen: *Poplar Trees*
Psalm 1:3
John 4:14
John 7:38

Chapter Fourteen: *A Time for Everything*
Ecclesiastes 3:1
1 Timothy 3:2–4
1 Corinthians 3:10

Epilogue: *The Treasures in My Bag*
Luke 10:3
Revelation 21:2–3
John 20:21

Printed in the United States
45471LVS00003B/1-153